ARE THERE YET?

TIPS AND TALES FROM A "FULL TIMING- PROFESSIONAL TOURIST"

BY

RANDY BADEAUX

Note for Librarians: a cataloguing record for this book that includes Dewey Decimal
Classification and US Library of Congress numbers is available from the Library and Archives
of Canada. The complete cataloguing record can be obtained from their online database at:
www.collectionscanada.ca/amicus/index-e.html
ISBN 1-4120-4437-5

TRAFFORD

Offices in Canada, USA, Ireland, UK and Spain
This book was published *on-demand* in cooperation with Trafford Publishing. On-demand
publishing is a unique process and service of making a book available for retail sale to the
public taking advantage of on-demand manufacturing and Internet marketing. On-demand
publishing includes promotions, retail sales, manufacturing, order fulfilment, accounting and
collecting royalties on behalf of the author.
Book sales for North America and international:
Trafford Publishing, 6E–2333 Government St.,
Victoria, BC v8t 4p4 CANADA
phone 250 383 6864 (toll-free 1 888 232 4444)
fax 250 383 6804; email to orders@trafford.com
Book sales in Europe:
Trafford Publishing (uk) Ltd., Enterprise House, Wistaston Road Business Centre,
Wistaston Road, Crewe, Cheshire cw2 7rp UNITED KINGDOM
phone 01270 251 396 (local rate 0845 230 9601)
facsimile 01270 254 983; orders.uk@trafford.com
Order online at:
www.trafford.com/robots/04-2245.html

10 9 8 7 6 5 4 3

Table of Contents

To my wife June,

Who smiled and went along with all this!

Introduction

My wife and I started Recreational Vehicle camping (RVing) in 1975 in a used tent trailer that I had to rebuild before we could use it. We didn't have a lot of money at the time and without the 'Pop-Up' we wouldn't have been able to afford to go anywhere. We have since had two brand new tent trailers, a 25 foot, High Low trailer, a 16 foot, and a 28 foot travel trailer and a 34 foot motor home.

I retired after being a Police Officer for twenty five years. We moved out of our house, sold all of our furniture and moved into the 28 foot, travel trailer that we had at the time. We were off on a great adventure in spite of the fact that a lot of friends and some of the family thought that we had gone off the deep end! We ignored them and became *"Professional Tourists"* or *"Full Timers"* as some call us.

In the following chapters I want to share with you some of the wonderful places we have been, the people we met, the great things we have done, some of the things that happened to us along the way and a few tips to make your travel easier.

So pull a lawn chair up next to the campfire, pour yourself a cup of coffee and come along on our adventures!

Randall Badeaux

Chapter 1: Attention to Details!

Location: Somewhere in Southern Louisiana

I did not witness the following event, but my Dad, who has since passed away, swore it was the truth until the day he died.

A young couple with two children pulled up into the campground with their 'Pop-Up' trailer. (a 'Pop Up' is a tent trailer where the upper canvas tent portion folds up and is stored in the bottom portion of the trailer for travel.) The man was driving and backed his trailer into the campsite, got out, unhooked the trailer from his car and began setting up the unit. He cranked the tent portion of the trailer up and pulled the beds out. (They generally pull out of both ends of the trailer.) He fastened the elastic cords that keep the canvas taunt. He pulled down his leveling jacks and carefully made sure that the trailer was level. He plugged in the electric cord and was all set, or so he thought.

There were two bicycles in a rack on top of the car. He took them down and each one of the children took a bike and they were off amidst the warnings of, "Watch out for cars," and "Be careful!" and "Have fun."

The man and the woman went into the camper and closed the door. All was quiet and serene on the campground.

After a little time had passed, suddenly one of the beds on the end of the camper came crashing down! The man and the woman both tumbled out of the camper off the broken bed onto the ground. **THEY WERE BOTH AS NAKED AS THE DAY THEY WERE BORN!!!**

The man jumped up and ran to the door of the camper. **LOCKED! *(of course!)*** He ran back to the end of the camper where the bed had fallen out and where his wife was doing everything possible to try to cover herself up! He scrambled up into the camper on the bed and in seconds had the door opened, his wife in the camper and the campground was once again quiet and serene.

After about ten minutes the man and woman again appeared. They immediately began to fold down the trailer. He lifted the leveling jacks and pushed both of the beds back into the unit. He cranked down the canvas portion of the trailer after unplugging the electric wire. The man and the woman hurriedly tucked in the canvas and latched down the roof. He hooked the trailer to the car and anxiously looked around for the children.

A few minutes later the children came by on their bikes. The parents flagged them down and told them they were leaving. There were a lot of protests from the children as the man put the bicycles back into the bike rack on the roof of the car.

"Why are we leaving? Where are we going? We just got here! Aren't we staying for the weekend?"

All complaints being duly noted the children were loaded into the car and the family sped off in a cloud of dust!

Now when you pull out the beds in a 'Pop-Up' camper there are usually two steel rods that fit between the outer edge of the bed and fasten into the frame of the trailer. In this case the man, obviously being in a hurry, forgot to put the bed braces in place, but, I'll bet he never-ever forgot about those braces again! *Pay attention to the details!*

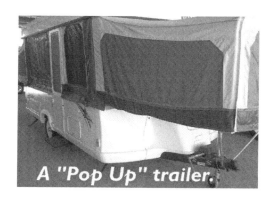

A "Pop Up" trailer.

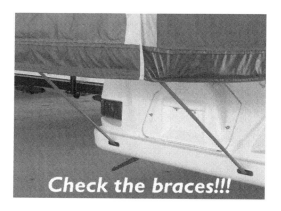

Check the braces!!!

Chapter 2: Our First RV

Location: Morgan City, Louisiana

I bought a used Starcraft tent trailer (we called it a 'Pop Up') in 1975. I had to take the canvas completely off of the rig and bring it to an upholstery shop to get the holes in all four corners patched. I had to repack the wheel bearings, paint the frame and scrub the walls and floors. Finally after several weekends of repair we were ready to go on our first trip.

We could have taken our maiden voyage on a weekend trip to a nearby campground but, I was hesitant to go because my wife had absolutely no experience in the outdoors and neither of us had ever camped in any type of R.V. We had planned a trip to Florida for our first ever vacation and I thought that if we took a weekend trip and it didn't go well, or if she decided that she didn't like camping, then the vacation would be off.

Finally the day arrived and we headed down the road with our Pop-Up trailer following our Toyota Corolla smartly down the highway. (Toyota cars were much, much smaller then and if you came up behind our trailer on the highway you couldn't see the car, so you thought that the trailer was going down the road by itself!).

Think Before You Act

Location: Styx River Resort, Mobile, Alabama)

We arrived at our first campground. It was a KOA just outside Mobile, Alabama.

We 'popped-up' the trailer and hooked up the electric and water lines and we were camping. A heavy (and I do mean **_heavy_** as it rains only on the Gulf Coast) rain storm came up. We immediately went inside and zipped up all the canvas and were sitting there looking at each other while the rain pounded the roof so hard we could hardly hear each other talk.

Then my wife had a great idea! As long as we were sitting there doing nothing anyway, why not start cooking dinner! I thought it was a great idea too. She got out the food and the pots and fired up our two burner built in propane stove. In about five minutes the temperature inside the little tent trailer was headed up to about 150!

It was an older model trailer and there was no roof vent and we didn't have any air conditioner! It was still raining so hard that we didn't dare un-zip any of the canvas. My wife said that if she turned off the stove, it would ruin our dinner. We sat and we sweated! (Perspired for you upper crust folks)

I don't remember whether she finished cooking first, or if the rain let up first, but we did learn a valuable lesson in cooking that day. **_Don't cook, don't even look at the cooking stove in a_**

tent trailer with all the canvas zipped up!!! (Unless you like sauna baths, of course.)

We had a lot of things to learn about camping. We didn't have a problem on every trip. In fact we enjoyed a lot of trouble free weekend jaunts and vacations, but I'd like to tell you some of the things that did happen to us. We were unaware that we had enrolled in 'Camping 101' at 'R V Travel University.'

Chapter 3: Check the Latches

Location: Highway 90 west of Franklin, Louisiana

It's Good to Know Your Equipment

We packed up our little 'Pop-Up' camper and headed down the road. I don't know if the latches that hold the roof secured for traveling worked their way loose, or if possibly I may have forgotten to properly adjust and check them, but any way we were headed up the highway. Our trailer was towing perfectly behind our Toyota Corolla and we were cruising along doing about fifty-five.

We were about twenty-five miles from home when all of a sudden, without warning, my car felt like I had slammed on the brakes. I quickly looked down at my instrument panel to see if I could detect any trouble. I saw immediately that our speed was down to about thirty!

I glanced in my rear view mirror and saw that the roof latches had come undone and the wind had caught in the canvas on the trailer and had pushed the roof almost all the way up! I was pulling a giant parachute behind the car.

I pulled over and got out of my car and walked back to the trailer. I started tucking the canvas in and letting the top back down trying to act casual, as if I often stopped on the side of a busy highway and inspected all the canvas on our 'Pop-Up'.

It didn't seem to have hurt anything and we continued on our trip after I adjusted the roof latches to their proper position. (I could hardly open the latches at the campground because they were so well adjusted.)

Camping Tip: Always try to find out all you can about your equipment. The dealer and service man are not always there ready to take care of your needs. Most of us want to get out of the city and into the beautiful countryside. The more things you can take care of yourself, the better off you will be. I always bring the manuals furnished with the RV and all the RV appliances with me when I travel. They have served me time and again in correcting problems.

The more you use your equipment, the more you will learn about it.

Chapter 4: The Furnace: A Love and Hate Relationship

We took our used trailer on our first vacation to Florida. We saw Silver Springs, spent time in St. Augustine, and went to Disney World for the first time. (Only the Magic Kingdom was opened then) We had a wonderful time and all of us in the family were hooked on camping. We really enjoyed the campgrounds with all the friendly people and for us it was the most economical way to travel. I mean we could fix our own meals, if we wanted to. We could cook outside, let the kids run wild and just relax and thoroughly enjoy ourselves. Don't get too excited now. We really didn't let the kids run too wild!

One piece of equipment I had in our 'Pop-Up' was a heating furnace. Now we had never camped in cold weather. Living in southern Louisiana we didn't really give a lot of thought to camping in winter, since our winters are usually very mild. It is not uncommon to wear short sleeved shirts on Christmas day.

Although I really didn't expect to use the heating furnace, I always lit the pilot light and made sure the furnace was working properly each time we took a trip. When I was getting ready, even for a weekend trip, I would always check the furnace. It always fired right up and worked great.

Location: KOA Campground, Lafayette, Louisiana

We decided to go on a three day weekend trip on the spur of the moment. I came home from work, hooked up the trailer to our little Toyota and took off. Lafayette was about seventy-five miles from our home.

We arrived at the campground and set everything up and were having a great time. Later that night a cold front came through. The temperature dropped to twenty-five degrees. I know that to some of you twenty-five degrees above zero does not sound cold, but in south Louisiana where the humidity is almost always high and where we are not used to cold weather, twenty-five degrees is **COLD!** Especially when you are staying in a glorified tent.

No problem. I got out of bed, plugged in the coffee pot and lit the burners on the stove to warm the place up. (I know that you are <u>not</u> supposed to use the stove for heating, but this was 1975 and I didn't know any better.)

When the place warmed up and I got back out of bed and put my clothes on, I tried to light the furnace. The pilot light lit just fine ...then.....**NOTHING HAPPENED!** The gas burner on the heating furnace would not come on. I didn't know what to do. I mean I had checked this furnace twenty times in the past and it worked fine. I hadn't checked it before we left this time because I hadn't taken the time to do it. We were in a hurry to get to the campground.

After checking everything that I knew how to check, I determined it must be the propane regulator. My Dad, who was camping with us in his own 'Pop-Up' trailer agreed with me, so it was off to town to get a new regulator. I didn't by a cheap regulator either. I bought the super-duper adjustable model that cost twice as much as the regular replacement. I went back to the trailer and put on the new regulator. Once inside, with blue fingers from the cold, *(no real man in Louisiana wears gloves in cold weather)* I lit the pilot light again. **NOTHING HAPPENED!**

I couldn't believe it. My furnace would not work. I spent the entire weekend trying to find the furnace trouble. I never could correct the problem. After a very cold trip, we went home.

When the weather warmed up again, I went out on my driveway determined to correct the problem I was having with the heating furnace. I checked everything again and again. I finally figured out that it was not a problem in the propane regulator since the cooking stove worked just fine. It had worked fine before I bought that new regulator. Finally I decided to take the furnace out and bring it to a repairman. I didn't know how to disconnect the furnace and pull it out of the unit for repair. I went inside and got a flashlight so I could see how to disconnect the outside vent. I turned on the light and shinned it into the pipe that goes from the furnace through the wall to the outside and supplies the furnace with fresh air. I saw one of the largest wasp's nests that I have ever seen blocking the pipe!

After cleaning that wasp nest out of the vent pipe, the heating furnace worked just fine. I checked it out thoroughly before each camping trip. I traded that camper off on a brand new tent trailer without ever using that furnace again.

Camping Tip: Do not use the stove burners for heating your RV. It is possible to get carbon monoxide poisoning. Use the built in furnace or get a good quality electric heater to do the job. Your electric heater should have a tip over shut off switch. If the heater gets accidentally tipped over, it will shut itself off automatically for safety.

I bought a 16 foot Jayco Songbird travel trailer. It had a brand new furnace in it. The first time I tried to use it, the pilot light would light, and then nothing would happen! I did all kinds of things trying to make that furnace work, but it never would.

I traded that camper in on a twenty-eight foot Coachmen travel trailer. The furnace worked fine in it, but over the eight years I kept that trailer I had to change the circuit board in the furnace twice. (Over a hundred dollars each time!) It didn't take me long to find out how to take the furnace out of the RV and fix it myself. (It's not that hard.) The first time I decided to 'do it myself' I got out the furnace manual and after some study started taking the furnace apart. There were wires hooked up in a lot of different places. I took my video camera and took about 30 seconds of video tape of those wires. When I went to reassemble everything, I reviewed the video tape, put it on 'pause' and replaced all the wires correctly. The furnace worked beautifully after putting in the new circuit board.

I have had to repair one of the furnaces in my Bounder Motor home. It was just a sensor switch, but the furnace won't work without it. In spite of the trouble these appliances have given me over the years, I still love to have a furnace when the weather turns cold!!!

Our furnaces in the Coachmen travel trailer and in our Bounder Motor home kept us warm and cozy through five winters in Alaska, in temperatures as low as -20 degrees.

Chapter 5: Floods

Location: A campground just west of Charleston, South Carolina

One summer, around the first part of June we took our 'Pop-Up' camper on vacation. We traveled to Tennessee, Kentucky, Virginia and then headed south through North and South Carolina on I-95. We stopped in a campground just to the west of Charleston, South Carolina, set up in our camping spot and were off to see the sights. We went out to Fort Sumter and saw the Battery and did a little shopping and then returned to our 'tent away from home'.

All was well. After a very enjoyable day we crawled into bed for a good nights sleep. Then the rain began. It rained and rained and rained all night. Somewhere close to daylight the rain stopped and we just stayed in bed and rested up. I was planning to head farther south, toward Florida that day.

I got out of bed and got the coffee pot going and got dressed. I couldn't see outside because the canvas walls were all zipped up on the trailer. After I dressed and got the rest of the family up and moving around and as soon as everyone was decent, I unzipped the canvas window that was located behind the dinner table.

I looked out and *I could not see any land!* We were parked in a lake! As far as I could see the campground was under water! I immediately started checking the trailer to see if any water was coming in through the floor. Thank God all was dry.

After a lot of coffee and a lot of looking out the windows it was time to try to get out of there. I rolled up my pants legs and took off my shoes and socks and stepped outside into the water. The water was about ten inches deep and it was cold! I walked to the back of the new pick-up truck that I had bought to tow the trailer and retrieved a pair of knee high rubber boots that I had stored in the back of the truck. I waded back to the trailer and dried off my feet and put my socks and those boots on and then went outside and started getting things ready to leave.

I don't mind telling you that I did not like disconnecting our electric cord while standing in that water! I carried our youngest son, who was about six years old at the time and put him in the truck. My wife, shoeless, waded through the cold water and got in the truck. I folded down the trailer and hooked it up to the truck and slowly pulled through the campground. After driving through the exit gate and going about a hundred yards up the road we were on dry ground again!

Location: Five Star Resort, Pass Christian, Mississippi

I pulled my twenty-eight foot Coachman travel trailer to Five Star Resort in Pass Christian, Mississippi and parked right next to a creek that runs through one side of the campground. My youngest son had driven over to meet us and to camp with us for the weekend. We really enjoyed ourselves in spite of the fact that it had been raining the entire time. Our Coachmen was nice and warm and cozy and we went to bed and all had a good nights sleep. I woke up in the morning and made a pot of coffee and was sitting at the dining table when I happened to look out of the window at the creek. The water in the creek was higher than I had ever seen it before and we had camped numerous times in this same spot. I made remarks to my son and my wife about how high the water was and then just went about my coffee drinking business.

A while later I looked out at the creek again and saw that the water **WAS COMING UP OUT OF ITS BANKS!** Realizing that now was **NOT** the time to panic; I calmly advised everyone that we should hook up and leave. **NOW!**

We got everything in the trailer ready to go. I went outside and disconnected electric wires and water hoses, etc. I backed up our Cheverolet Suburban and hooked up the trailer hitch and the safety chains and plugged in the trailer lights.

Camping Tip: Please! Try Not to Panic!

I had an electric jack on the trailer hitch that raised and lowered the front of the trailer by pressing a button instead of cranking it up and down by hand. I pressed the button on the hitch and it **WOULD NOT DO ANYTHING!** I checked the wire from the hitch that went to the battery and it was all right. I checked the fuse and it was O.K. I tried to make that jack work every way I knew how. I must have pressed that button on the front of the jack until I almost smashed it in! It still would not work. I could hear the motor in the jack running, but nothing was happening. I got out my toolbox and took the plate off the top of the jack and soon discovered that there was a steel pin that held the gears in place and it had sheared off! Not having another pin to replace it with, I decided to just take the jack off and go home and worry about it when I was safely parked in my high and dry driveway. THE CREEK WAS STILL RISING! The water was just a few feet from my camper.

There were just three bolts that fastened the jack to the trailer frame. I got a wrench and soon had the three bolts out. **THE JACK WOULDN'T MOVE!** It was jammed in the frame of the trailer! I got a hammer and tapped it all around. Nothing doing! I couldn't just drive off because the jackleg was extended down to the ground. (I really thought about driving off anyway) I was starting to get really upset. I beat on the jack harder with the hammer, but that didn't do any good. Then ... **HELP** arrived.

I looked up because someone was speaking to me, asking if I needed help. There were three senior citizen type guys that were parked farther up the hill. I told them the problem and they immediately started telling me how to get the jack off the trailer frame. Unfortunately they all had a different idea about how to go about it. I even thought they were going to get in an argument amongst themselves about how to get me out of my dilemma. **I started really beating the devil out of that jack with my hammer!** It didn't do any more good than before. THE CREEK WAS STILL RISING AND THE WATER WAS ALMOST AT MY DOOR!

Finally I got an idea. I got a pipe wrench out of my tool box, adjusted it to fit the base of the jack and tried to turn the jack to free it. One of the guys said, "Turn it to the right." Another said, "No, don't turn it to the right, turn it to the left." The third old guy said, "Try beating it with the hammer again!" The jack wouldn't budge an inch. I went back to the toolbox and looked into it expecting some miracle tool to appear. It didn't. The three *"helpers"* were still discussing how to go about helping me. In the end, I stuck a piece of pipe on the pipe wrench handle and with the extra leverage the jack finally came free!

I thanked the three good Samaritans, threw the broken jack into the back of the Suburban and told my wife to get in. My son had already left when we said we were getting out of the campground and he had missed all the fun!

I cranked up the engine and started up the hill. The rear wheels on the Suburban lost traction on the wet clay street and I couldn't get up the hill! I won't even tell you the cuss words that went through my mind, but I didn't holler them out because the three good Samaritans were still closely watching me! **Then they came to the rescue!** All three of them pushed the

25

Suburban while I drove and in just a moment we were up the hill and safe from the still rising waters of the creek.

I drove home and ordered another steel pin and fixed the jack when it came in.

That Jack Finally Cranked Me Up!

Location: Hacienda RV Resort, Las Vegas, Nevada

The jack broke in Louisiana and again in St. David, Arizona. I fixed it both times and it broke again the fourth time at the Hacienda campground in Las Vegas. *(It has since be blown up!)*

I had our travel trailer backed into the rather short campsite that I was assigned to. I was towing with a Chevy Suburban and the Suburban was out in the street and blocking up one lane of traffic. I unhooked the safety chains and the trailer light plug and when I attempted to lower the leg on the electric jack it did nothing but sit there and hum! Enough was enough! I got out the tool box, took off the electric jack and reinstalled the hand crank jack that I had carefully stored in one of the outside storage boxes on the trailer after the ordeal on the creek bank. With the hand crank jack in place, I was able to unhook the trailer and get the Suburban off the street.

The last time I saw that jack was when I threw it into the trash bin in Las Vegas! I used a muscle powered hand crank jack, which was still on the front end of that trailer when I traded it in. Sometimes modern and easier is not necessarily better.

Yes, It Will Flood in the Desert!

Location: In the desert at Quartzsite, Arizona

We were camped in the desert just south of Quartzsite, Arizona. We had attended the giant flea market there. I don't know if you've ever been to Quartzsite around the end of January and the first week or so of February, but it is really something to see. It's the biggest flea market I've ever seen. You can buy anything from false teeth to an airplane! There is everything you ever heard of for sale and a lot of things you've probably never heard of for sale too.

Well any way, the flea market had wound down, but we just stayed camping there in the desert. We had bought a camping pass from the Bureau of Land Management that was good for six months and we were getting our money's worth. I had also been doing a little gold panning and we were having a great time. The desert is so beautiful. I spent a lot of time just walking out among the cactuses, kicking rocks and just enjoying myself. You have to remember that a desert is a curious place to a Cajun that was raised in the swamps of south Louisiana.

We were parked about a mile off the main road. I had unhitched our Coachmen twenty-eight foot trailer from our

27

Chevy Suburban. It started to rain. It rained harder and harder. I was really amazed to see so much rain in the desert. It rained and rained and rained and rained. I sat looking out the window and then I saw it. It was like a river that sprang out of the ground. A roaring, foaming, gushing river of brown muddy water washing through the gully that was about fifty yards from my camper! I kept looking at the newly formed river as it got deeper and angrier and faster. The muddy water foamed as it rolled and tumbled to its unknown destination, all the while making an angry roaring sound. I felt as if I had to do something so I went outside in the rain. The rain had slacked some, but it was still a steady downpour. I decided to hook the travel trailer up in case I had to hurry to get out of there.

I backed the Chevy up to the trailer and hooked everything up and made ready to leave. Then I started looking around. *There were rushing, roaring, rivers of water completely surrounding us!*

The rain was slacking off now and I was very thankful, but I still didn't know how much the water was going to rise. All we could do was wait and pray! The rain quit. We waited. After about an hour, I could see that the water was going down. The rivers were calming down (and so was I!) and didn't look as enraged any more. Then within a few hours...*ALL OF THE WATER WAS GONE!*

It was almost as if the rain had never fallen. The earth had opened her mouth and swallowed all that water!

Well, since I was all hooked up, I drove toward town and finally parked in a place that looked to me like it was higher ground. We were OK and nothing was harmed.

Even to this day, when I pull into a campground, or if we're 'boon-docking' out in the wilderness somewhere, I still check around to see if we are on high ground. I have a campground membership at Mill Creek Resort in Pigeon Forge, Tennessee and when I register there I always ask the clerk, "Could I please get up on top of the hill?"

An Internal Flood

Location: An RV Park just south of New Iberia, Louisiana

My Mom and Dad bought a 'Pop-Up' trailer back in the '70s. My Dad was really enthusiastic about having the trailer and my Mom sort of thought my Dad was 'nuts'. She couldn't understand why a person would want to go to a campground when there were perfectly good hotel rooms near by. So Dad came home with the new 'Pop-Up' and they loaded a few groceries into it and off they went on their first adventure.

They drove about fifty miles and got into the only camp ground that Dad knew about in our area and started 'setting up'. It didn't take long for some of the other campers to come over and give him all sorts of 'pointers' on how to set up the trailer, since it was probably very obvious that this was something new and foreign to them. They were so new to camping that they hadn't even brought any lawn chairs to sit outside and had to go down to the friendly K-Mart store and purchase some.

After a pleasant day of camping and my Dad doing a lot of talking trying to convince my Mom just how great camping really was and how much fun they were having, they retired to bed.

In the morning my Dad awoke. The sun was shinning brightly, the birds were singing! Dad swung his feet over the side of the bed and into **WATER!** The water was a foot deep inside of the camper! His bedroom slippers were floating!

He yelled at Mom, "Get up! Get up! We're in a flood!" He quickly put his clothes on and ran to the door and opened it. Water gushed forth from the camper door. The campground was completely **DRY!** Expecting to see everything under water, Dad was even more shocked!

Upon investigation it was found that a 'flap valve' had failed to perform and stop the water from going into the fresh water tank as it was supposed to do. The water tank, being made of plastic, had swelled to about twice its original size and had ruptured. The water hose was still filling the trailer with gallons and gallons of water!

The dealer replaced the valve and the water tank and they never had any trouble like that again. My Mom was convinced that camping was a great thing and I believe she fell in love with camping even more that he did.

Camping Tip: Check Out the Lay of the Land BEFORE You Set Up! You might want to check out the weather report also so you can get an idea of what to expect. Try not to camp in apparently low lying areas if lots of rain is expected.

Check out the creek, river, pond or lake. Ask questions when checking in, especially if it has been raining, or has rained a lot in the last few days or if lots of rain is expected and if the creek, etc. is prone to rise dramatically after rain. I have had to move our RVs twice since these other incidents because of lakes rising after lots of rain.

Chapter 6: Brakes and Towing
Please! Let Me Go!

Location: Interstate 10 exit at Spanish Fort, Alabama

I towed my first 'Pop-Up' trailer with a Toyota Corolla. The car was much smaller than the trailer. If you came up behind the trailer while we were going down the highway, you could not see the car. People would pass us up and look and look at that tiny car. I guess they thought the trailer was going down the road by itself!

The trailer had a surge brake. Now, a surge brake is a contraption hooked up to the front of the trailer tongue and it applies pressure to the trailer brakes when you start stopping the tow vehicle. The harder you stop the tow vehicle, the harder the pressure this puts on the trailer tongue and the more pressure is applied to the trailer brakes. This is a great invention and with our very small Toyota, I probably would not have been able to stop the trailer with out assistance from that brake. It really worked great! I would be towing down the highway and would need to stop. I would start braking and you could immediately feel the trailer push on the back end of the car, and then the surge brake would kick in and it was as though the trailer wasn't even there.

On our first out of town trip we were headed to Florida. Now this was before I-10 was opened all the way and you had to get on and off the interstate highway several times between Louisiana and I-75 in Florida. On one of the detours I had to come down a very steep hill and at the bottom of the hill was a traffic signal. The light turned red and I stopped the rig with no trouble. I had to make a left turn when the light changed. Now being on a steep hill and still facing down the incline, I didn't realize it at the time, but the trailer was pushing on the rear bumper and the trailer brakes were activated!

The traffic signal turned green and I started to go. My car was a standard shift. I had the transmission in first gear. I pressed the gas pedal and let up on the clutch and then the car would not go. More gas and **NOTHING GOING!**

There is that split second when you think, "This is it! The car in not going! We are stuck here in the middle of the road! How am I going to unlock those brakes? How many cars are behind me and wanting to know who the dummy is up ahead sitting here through the green light! Do something! **DO SOMETHING!!!**"

All I did was push the clutch back in, give the car a lot more gas and then sort of 'pop' the clutch. The car moved a little and took the pressure off the surge brake and then we proceeded down the road. No problem!

I know that this is really nothing, but if you have ever towed …anything…down the highway, then you know that some weird things can come across your mind about that …whatever it is

...that you're dragging behind you. Those brakes worked fine and when I traded that 'Pop-Up' trailer in on a new one; I paid extra to have surge brakes on it too.

Check Out that Hitch!

Location: Highway 90 in Southern Louisiana

I finally had to get another tow vehicle. After towing my first two trailers a lot of miles, I was headed down the highway going home and I kept hearing this, "BLONK.....BLONK....BLONK". I pulled over twice and checked out the trailer hitch and running gear and couldn't see anything. Then we wouldn't hear anything for a while and then, "BLONK....BLONK.....BLONK!" I couldn't figure out what that sound was. I drove home and parked the rig with no trouble and the next day I got out and started looking around to see if I could find the trouble.

First of all I checked the trailer. I even got up under it and checked out all the running gear and couldn't find anything wrong, so I started checking the trailer hitch on the rear of the Toyota. I opened the trunk and moved the spare tire so I could see where the trailer hitch was bolted on. The dealership had put the trailer hitch on for me and I thought I was in real good shape, but the way the trailer hitch was made it was bolted through the thin metal sheeting that made up the floor of the trunk. I saw a four inch long split in the metal floor where the bolts of the trailer hitch came up through the floor! The Lord was with us, I can guarantee! There must have been an angel back there holding that trailer onto the back of the car, because the trailer hitch sure wasn't doing very much to hold it on!

Later, when I towed with a Ford pick-up and after that with a Chevrolet Suburban, I can't tell you how many times I got under those vehicles to check the trailer hitches!

Camping Tip: You need to crawl up under your tow vehicle and check the hitch. Make sure all the nuts and bolts are tight and that the hitch is very securely attached to the vehicle frame. Make sure that the trailer hitch ball is tight and secure.

The trailer tongue and rear bumper of the tow vehicle should be level. If the trailer tongue is not level it will cause steering problems and possibly and accident.

After hooking up, remember to make sure that all running lights and tail lights are working properly. Make sure you check those turn signals and brake lights too.

Chapter 7: Balance

Location: Yogi Bear RV Resort, Robert, Louisiana

You Get What You Pay For

One Easter weekend we met my Mom and Dad for a camping get together. It was a beautiful weekend with great weather and we really had a good time. Now my Dad liked to drink beer and he was really a connoisseur of beer. He always bought the **cheapest** one!

Well, my dad came out of his 'Pop-Up' camper and had a can of beer in his hand. He pulled the tab and opened the beer and then sat down in his lawn chair. The arms of the chair bent up in the middle and **that chair crashed down in a tangled heap!** It came apart like a two-dollar suit!

My Dad was sitting flat on the ground on top of the chair and he was still holding that can of beer. He held it out at the end of his arm like a man trying to balance on a tight wire. He looked at the beer totally ignoring the crushed up lawn chair and said, "Never spilled a drop!" The trouble with Dad was that he had the same taste in lawn chairs as he did in beer. He always bought the **cheapest** one!

8: Be Prepared For Anything

Indoor Rain

Location: Corps of Engineer Campground, Des Moines, Iowa.

I bought a Coleman 'Pop Up' camper. It was a nice trailer and had a queen sized bed on one end. I had a Buick Park Avenue that I was towing with.

We took a trip up into Iowa for a shooting match. I was a police officer and spent a lot of time shooting in competition and the Police National Championships were in Iowa that year. We towed up to Des Moines and stayed in a beautiful spot at the Corp of Engineers campground right near the dam.

I didn't win the championship, but we had a good time anyway. We were camped at the dam and I had a 5,000 BTU air conditioner that fit in a frame on the side of the trailer after it was 'popped up'. We went to bed one night and went right to sleep and had a wonderful night's sleep. *I was awakened by water dripping in my face!* I thought at first that it was raining and I had sprung a leak in the canvas over the bed. Wrong! It was a beautiful sunny day outside.

I sat up in bed and saw that water was dripping all over the inside of the camper! It took a few moments to try to get my brain into focus. Then it dawned on me what was happening. The air conditioner had made it a lot colder inside the trailer than it was outside, (of course that is what it is supposed to do) but, the cold air had formed condensation on the inside of the canvas. It was literally raining on the inside of the camper while it was a nice sunny day on the outside!

After shutting the air conditioner off and unzipping all the canvas it wasn't very long before it all dried out. We left the roof vent (this camper had one) open at night and that seemed to help things out.

Camping Tip: Be prepared! Just Like the Boy Scouts say:
For anything!

Location: I-59 South of Birmingham, Alabama

After I left Iowa we went down to Chattanooga, Tennessee for a few days of sliding down the Alpine Slide at the Raccoon Mountain campground and then headed back home to Louisiana.

I was headed south on I-59 between Birmingham and Tuscaloosa, Alabama. It was a beautiful Sunday and we were enjoying the trip, looking forward to getting home, when all of a sudden the steering wheel started to vibrate and I heard a loud sound, almost like a roaring coming from the back of the car. It looked like the radio was trying to vibrate out of the dashboard. I had blown a tire on the trailer!

I pulled off on the side of the interstate highway, got out and checked the damage. The driver side trailer tire was in shreds! Of course I didn't have a spare tire for the trailer. I had never needed one before. I got my jack out of the back of the Buick and took the tire off the trailer and put it in the trunk of the Buick. I told my wife to go down the interstate to the next gas station or whatever and have a new tire mounted while I stayed with the trailer. It was an odd sized tire that fit on that Coleman, a Michelin 8.00 X 10.00.

I sat on the side of the interstate drinking hot Cherry Cool Aid and watching the traffic go by. In about an hour my wife came back. She advised me that no one had a tire this size. She had gone to Tuscaloosa and had checked several places and no one had anything even close to replacing the blown tire.

I got in the car with my wife and son and we headed back up to Birmingham. I checked every place that looked like it might sell tires, but to no avail. My choices were limited since it was Sunday. I pulled into a gas station, deli-grocery store on the west end of Birmingham and told the man what I needed. He told me he was a personal friend of the man that ran the tire manufacturing company of the kind of tire I needed and the factory was right here in Birmingham. He got the man on the telephone and he informed me that he could have a tire for me in *six to eight weeks!* He told me they only make one size tire at a time and the size I needed would be produced again in six to eight weeks and he didn't know of any dealer that would stock that size tire!

The man at the gas station was nice. He made a new pot of coffee and we put most of it into our thermos bottle and we bought some sandwiches, cookies and a bunch of other snacks and went back to the trailer that was still sitting on the side of I-59 perched up on my scissors jack.

It was almost dark and we listened to cassette tapes for a while and we just sat and watched the traffic go by our window at 100 miles an hour! Every time a big truck passed us, it rocked the car back and forth. I was wondering if a good blast of wind from one of those trucks might knock the trailer off the jack. After a few hours our son stretched out on the back seat and went to sleep. I tilted the seat back as far as it would go and after a while I drifted off to sleep and although I woke up a few times during the night, I can say I really had a pretty good nights sleep. I found out that my wife, June had stayed awake all night *guarding* us! Wasn't that sweet!

Well, we got up and unable to brush our teeth or change clothes (all of our things were packed away in the trailer which was folded down) we headed to Tuscaloosa. After several stops at the tire stores we were informed, as before, that we were not going to be able to purchase a tire of that size. All of them wanted to order us a tire and we could probably get one in six to eight weeks.

I had an idea. I looked in the telephone book and found a dealer that sold boats and motors and **boat trailers.** I called him on the telephone and found out that he was close by. I drove over to his place.

I took the shredded tire out of the trunk and showed it to the man at the boat dealership. I told him what our problem was and he showed me another tire and rim. It was a different size, but he assured me that the load rating was sufficient to carry the weight of the trailer if I had enough clearance under the fender well. The tire was taller than the originals by a few inches. I bought two tires and rims and drove back to the trailer that was still on the side of I-59. I put one of the new tires on and it fit great with several inches of clearance under the fender well to spare. I was going to change both tires because of the size difference. When I took off the other tire (the one that I thought was still good) there was an egg in the tire the size of a soft ball! If I had had a spare for the trailer it wouldn't have done me any good. Within a few miles the other tire would have blown too!

I got back home and the tire dealer ordered me two new tires and they both arrived in about six or eight weeks. After that, not only did I have a spare tire, I had another set of tires! I always made sure I had a spare tire for the trailers I bought after that one. I have never had another tire problem on the road with any of our travel trailers and that includes trips up and down the Alaska Highway.

I did blow a our tire on our motor home coming through Kansas. Of course it was an inside rear tire. I called our road service insurance on the cell phone and a repairman was soon dispatched to change the tire.

Camping Tip: Purchase a good tire gage and check the air pressure in your tires on a regular basis. An under-inflated tire will cause tread wear on both edges of the tire and can get hot and blow out, causing damage to the vehicle or even cause an accident. The air pressure required for the tires is printed on the tire sidewall. Over-inflated tires will cause them to wear out prematurely down the center of the tires tread and can cause a blow out as well. Keep them at the proper inflation level. Make sure you have the proper tires for the load you expect them to carry. Check with your local tire dealer for information on which is the best tire for your rig.

Get some good road service insurance. It is a wonderful thing when you have a problem on the road to know that you can call and get help and don't have to have a pocket full of money to shell out right on the side of the highway. There are several plans available out there. Good Sam Club offers a plan that we subscribe to and the two times I have had to call them for road service they were great.

Location: State Park Campground, Grand Isle, Louisiana

Air Conditioning

We had planned a trip to Grand Isle, Louisiana to do some surf fishing. It was in the summer time and south Louisiana in the summer time is HOT! I took the Coleman trailer to a man that could install the air conditioner in a permanent location. Putting that heavy air conditioner up in the rack on the side of the camper had gotten the best of my back and I wanted it mounted in a place out of the way and somewhere where I didn't have to pick it up and take it down every time we set the camper up.

The workman made a lot of measurements and finally took a radial saw and cut a hole in the rear of the camper. The hole came out under the table inside the trailer. He made a frame and mounted the air conditioner. It was a really neat job and looked like a factory installation. It took him the better part of a day to do the work.

We towed down to Grand Isle and drove into the State Park there. We paid our fees and followed the directions to the camping area, which is right on the beach. We pulled up to a really beautiful spot. Then we noticed that there were **NO ELECTRIC HOOKUPS IN THE CAMPGROUND!**

I was really outdone! All the time and money I had spent fixing that air conditioner and now there was no electricity to run it.

We had a good time without the electricity anyway. We caught a lot of fish and crabs and had a wonderful time. I sold that Coleman trailer without ever using that air conditioner after I had it permanently installed.

Camping Tip: You might want to call the campground and find out just exactly what amenities they offer *before* you get there. Get a good campground directory. The amenities are listed for each park and you know what to expect upon arrival. It is always a good idea to be prepared in the event you have no electricity, water, sewer, etc.

We always carry a 12 volt fan which will run off the 12 volt electric system in our RV. (All of the lights will run off the RV battery also) That fan has helped us get cool nights sleep while out "boon docking". The fan only uses about 1 ½ amps per hour and is easy on our battery. You can find these fans at many camping and auto parts stores.

We also make sure that we have water in our fresh water tank in the event that no potable water is readily available.

Another good investment is a 12 volt to 110 volt power inverter. You can purchase them in different wattages, but I prefer one that I can plug into the cigarette lighter receptacle. These inverters come in handy if you want to plug in a lamp, charge the cell phone, video camera or computer battery or even watch TV. They are not expensive and really come in handy.

Chapter 9: New RV Trailers

Impulse Buying

I was in Baton Rouge, Louisiana on business with a friend and we just happened to stop at a camper dealership. We were looking through the units when I spotted a little (and I do mean little) sixteen foot Jayco Song Bird travel trailer. We went inside and looked around. It had a dinette table that converted into a double bed and a small sofa that also converted into a single bed. It had a two burner propane stove; a furnace and it also had a **BATHROOM!** Now as much as I like 'Pop Up' trailers I had never seen one with a bathroom. *(Now some of the new models do have a bathroom in them!)* Although this was a very tiny bathroom, it still had all the good stuff, like a toilet and a shower! You could actually sit on the toilet and take a shower at the same time if you had a mind to, although I don't know of anyone who actually admitted to doing so.

The next thing I knew, I was in the office and had bought that trailer! Now I usually would never have purchased anything without my wife being there to supervise, but I knew in my heart that when she saw that little, tiny bathroom she would fall in love with it. So without any hesitation I bought that bathroom and the dealership went ahead and threw in the rest of the trailer for free!

I had so much fun buying the trailer, my friend couldn't resist and he bought one too! I'll bet that salesman is still wishing for two more guys like us to show up!

I left the trailer there for the dealership to service it and would return later to pick it up.

I couldn't wait to get home to tell my wife about our new trailer. She wasn't very enthusiastic about the whole thing. I guess it may have been partly because we still had the Coleman 'Pop Up' sitting in the front yard and we were still paying monthly notes on it.

I was still excited. I told her we would sell the Coleman and then the notes on the travel trailer would be about the same. Besides the Song Bird had a **BATHROOM!**

In a couple of days I went back to Baton Rouge and picked up our new trailer and towed it about seventy miles to our home. I pulled up in the front yard and my wife came out to see it. I unlocked the door and she stepped up into the trailer. She stood there for a few seconds and then said in a nervous voice, "I don't know if I can stay in here!" and then took off out the door and back out into the front yard. I had forgotten that my wife had been trapped in an elevator one time for several hours and she didn't like to be in small places and believe me the inside of that Song Bird was *small!*

I followed her into the yard and started pleading my case. "What do you mean you can't stay in there? **We** bought this trailer! It's ours! We have to pay for it. It has air conditioning. It has a stove. It has a furnace. **It has a BATHROOM!"**

In a few minutes she went back inside and everything seemed to be O.K. I mopped the sweat from my brow. All was well! I always made sure that all the curtains were opened and kept the door open when possible so that the inside of the little Song Bird would look as roomy and airy as possible.

Someone came by in a few days and bought our Coleman 'Pop Up' and we were again down to one camper payment per month. We ended up camping in that Song Bird for about four years.

Camping Tip: Be smarter than I was. Bring your spouse with you when you buy your RV. I'll say it again, *"BRING YOUR SPOUSE WITH YOU!"*

Our Florida Souvenir
Location: Winter Garden, Florida

We were on a winter vacation in Florida and we took a day to look at new camper trailers. The Song Bird had served us well, but we were interested in something that we could both fit in at one time. We had looked at several dealerships and had not found the 'right' one. We drove up north of Kissimmee on highway 50 and stopped at Giant R.V. They sold Coachmen products and we started looking at the trailers on their lot. It started pouring rain. We had an umbrella and we just kept on shopping. We had looked at about ten or twelve units and still didn't see anything that we just had to have. There was only one unit left to see and it was parked at the far end of the row. We hurriedly opened the door and went in. I walked to the rear of the trailer and saw the roomy bathroom that was built across the rear end of the unit. I turned around and was about to tell my wife that the trailer looked longer from the outside, when I noticed that there was a bedroom in the front of the trailer. That was a novelty to us at the time and we fell in love with it. The color scheme was mauve and blue and my wife loved it.

We walked back in the rain to the office and found a salesman. I told him that I wanted to know the price of the front bedroom travel trailer parked on the end of the row. He told me that Coachmen didn't make a front bedroom trailer. I gave him my umbrella and sent him out on the lot in the rain to see the rig for himself. He returned in a few minutes with a number written on his hand with a ball point pen telling us that he had never seen a Coachmen front bedroom trailer before.

To cut to the chase, we bought that trailer, trading in the Song Bird. I left my Chevy Suburban at the dealership to have all the wiring and trailer brakes checked out. They loaned us a Chevy dual wheeled pickup truck to use until the next day.

If You Have to Wait...Do it at Disney World

I called the salesman the next morning and he told us that our rig would be ready about four P.M. so we took the truck they loaned us and went to Disney World. We wondered around the Magic Kingdom trying to have fun, but all we could do was think about our new rig. Finally about three o'clock I called and they told me to come and get it.

Know the One "That Brung Ya"!

We walked outside the Magic Kingdom and boarded the tram going to the parking area. We got off at the lot where the borrowed truck had been parked. (The parking lots have names like Goofy, Mickey and Minnie, etc.) Then we started walking around trying to remember what kind of truck they had loaned us. We knew it was Chevy and we believed it was red and white, but we were not positively sure. After a few minutes of walking around the parking lot, I spied a dual wheeled, red and white Chevy truck. The key fit so we drove it off!

I went to the campground and hooked up the Song Bird and pulled it to Giant R.V. They had our new trailer all hooked up to the Suburban and after the customary walk through to show you how to use everything, I pulled the new Coachmen to the rear of their parking lot and then went back and pulled the Song Bird up door to door so we could unload our belongings from the Song Bird and into the new Coachmen.

Where Did All the Space Go?

We started unloading and loading, if you know what I mean. We found things in that Song Bird that we had not seen in four years! We moved 'stuff' and moved 'stuff'. Now our new Coachmen was a twenty-eight footer and the Song Bird, as I have said before was sixteen foot long. We had so much 'stuff' in the sixteen foot trailer that it seemed as though it wouldn't all fit in the new Coachmen! We had things stacked every where!

Finally we just piled a lot of stuff in the middle of the floor, on the sofa, the dinette, the bed and everywhere else that we could find an empty spot. If you have ever had any type of R.V. for a length of time you know how many things you can accumulate. We were no exception. Finally, the Song Bird was empty and I told the salesman that if he found anything in it that we had forgotten it was his, because we didn't know we had it anyway!

We pulled the trailer to the campground, about a twenty five mile trip. The trailer pulled like a dream and we arrived just about dark.

There is Always Plenty of Help

I was going to have to back the trailer into our spot. I had backed trailers in a lot of spots in the past, but this was a new rig and it was longer than any I had ever towed. I started to back the rig down. My wife was standing at the rear of the trailer guiding me as she always did. I was watching her in the rear view mirrors, when suddenly three senior citizen type guys appeared. They were from the surrounding campsites and they saw the new rig and believed it was their sworn duty to help us get the rig onto our site. I looked in the mirror on the driver's side and the man was telling me to swing the back end of the trailer to the right. I looked in the passenger door mirror and the man was trying to tell me to swing the back end of the trailer to the left! The third man was trying to tell the other two men what to signal! (These could have been the same three guys that helped me to get the jack off my trailer some years later in Mississippi!) [See the chapter on Floods]

After several attempts at backing in and getting farther and farther away from where I wanted to park, I stopped the Suburban and turned the engine off and got out of the cab. I walked around to see just exactly where I was trying to go. As I walked around, I noticed that the camping spot directly behind me was empty! I told those guys and my wife to, "Just stand by!"

I got back in the truck, fired it up and drove around the block. Once even with the site that was behind mine, I drove through and stopped on my own site! This won't work most of the time, but it sure worked that time. I was happy, my wife was happy and our three neighbors were happy.

I went ahead and disconnected the trailer from the truck, leveled it and hooked up the electric, water, etc. It took us about two days to find a place to stash everything. We spent months of moving things around to see where they fit the best. I want to tell you that moving into a new camper is HARD WORK!!!

Camping Tip: Consideration must be given as to where things are stored. You must attempt to store your load so that the vehicle will be balanced. I had a friend of mine that was planning to take his Class C motor home to the dealer because he noticed that the vehicle was leaning toward the passenger side about 3 or 4 inches lower than on the driver side. He mentioned this to me and I went with him to expect the rig. I found out that he had all his heavy gear stored on the passenger side of the motor home. All his canned goods, bottles, etc. were stored on the passenger side. The refrigerator was built in on this side, as well as his fresh water tank. By simply rearranging his load the problem was solved.

Another friend of mine was towing his travel trailer just outside of Seattle, Washington. He had stored a lot of heavy belongings inside the RV and at the rear end of the trailer. He soon found out that the trailer would not track well. (The trailer was trying to steer his truck.) After a few miles on the interstate the trailer got away from him and the trailer was totaled out!

He wasn't injured, thank God, but he had learned a very, very expensive lesson on proper weight distribution.

Loading a travel trailer properly will help the way it will tow. Too much load in the rear or over the trailer tongue can cause problems. Split the load up as evenly as possible around the rig and you can avoid a lot of problems on the road.

Our Coleman 'Pop Up' in Iowa

Camping in the Jayco Songbird in Louisiana

Chapter 10: The Shower House

Location: An RV Resort near Fort Mill, South Carolina

We had driven up to Fort Mill, South Carolina and were camping at the P.T.L. campground. It was a beautiful place and we were really having a good time camping in our Song Bird. Then the weather turned cold. The temperature was hovering in the teens, the humidity was up and it was just plain COLD!

I got up one morning and opted to go to the public bathhouse to shave. I grabbed all the shaving equipment I would need and stuffed it in a bag and headed to the shower house, which is just about three camping spaces down from where we were parked.

I walked in and found the place to be nice and warm and very clean. *(We have been in some bathhouses where we did not want to touch anything, if you know what I mean!)* I walked over to the lavatory and was preparing my things, when I noticed a man standing over in the corner of the room. He was just standing there looking around, not apparently doing anything, but being a cop and totally suspicious of everyone and everything, he just looked out of place to me.

I went about lathering up my face and getting my razor ready, but I kept an eye on this guy watching him in the mirror. He was just standing there, kind of looking around. Now I don't know anyone who goes on shower house sightseeing tours, unless something is wrong with him. The longer I stood there watching him in the mirror, the longer he just stood there looking around. The more he stood there, the more it seemed to me that he was out of place. Something was wrong, but I didn't know what. All kinds of things *(mostly weird)* were going through my mind. I couldn't help but wonder if this guy was some kind of a pervert that liked to hang around in bathrooms.

He just kept standing there and I noticed the look on his face. It was a sheepish, embarrassed look. A look that was telling me that he wished that I would not have come in.....like he was trying to hide something. This only made my level of suspicion soar!

Then he went over into a shower stall and I heard the water come on. I felt a little relieved thinking that he was just there to shower, but I was determined to keep an eye focused in his direction. I could see the steam coming up out of the shower stall when I looked back through the mirror.

I was just about finished shaving and I hadn't done a very good job of it. I was paying more attention to that guy than I was to my face. I still felt very uneasy about him being in there with me. I was hoping someone else would come in, but of course no one else did.

I was starting to gather my belongings so I could get out of there, when he opened the door to the shower stall and came out. He was still dressed. My suspicion alarm was going full blast! He walked back over to the corner of the shower house and leaned over and picked up a water hose that was lying on the floor. I hadn't noticed the hose before this. I guess I was so intent on watching him that I didn't pay any attention to anything else. The hose was as stiff as a board and with some difficulty he bent the hose in half and went back into the shower stall and stood the hose up against the wall to let the hot water splash down upon it.

He came out of the shower stall, still looking sheepish and embarrassed. He told me, "I was trying to leave the campground this morning, but my hose had frozen during the night and I couldn't wrap it up to make it fit in the storage box on my rig."

I was sure glad he had a good reason for the way he was acting. I was really glad that he wasn't a pervert as I had first suspected! Whenever I go in a shower house, I still look around to see what is going on and who is hanging around, but I never did see anyone else giving his water hose a shower!

Chapter 11: The Campfire

If you don't know how to spend good quality time with your kids, camping could be the answer. We started camping when our youngest was about five years old. If you like to see your kids having a good time in a wholesome environment and be able to have some fun with them, then I recommend the campground.

We have camped with the kids on rivers, lakes, in forests, on ponds, creeks, in the mountains, in the valleys, on the plains and in the hills. Each place has been a unique experience and has left us with many great memories.

We traveled to Belmont campground in New Iberia, Louisiana on one of our first weekend excursions. When it started getting dark I decided to build a campfire. I knew that our youngest son had never experienced a campfire and I couldn't wait to see his reactions. I had some small logs that I had brought with us and I gathered up a lot of fallen tree branches and twigs and whatever else I could find and piled them up and brought my Boy Scout education into play and soon had the fire blazing. I took one of the logs and set it by the fire and got my little one and sat him down on it. I told him that the cowboys always pulled up a log and sat around the campfire. I told him that the fire could burn him and that he was not to play in the fire, because it was dangerous and I didn't want him to get hurt. He sat there and looked into the fire, hypnotized by the flames, as so many of us have been. We let him roast marshmallows and he thought that was great.

My wife however, was a different story. Every time I looked around she was putting twigs on the fire, she was putting dried leaves on the fire, she was putting little pieces of paper in the fire. She was poking the fire with a stick and was constantly doing something to the fire. I didn't know it, but she had never seen or been around an open campfire before!

I told her the old proverb, "If you play in the fire too long, you'll wet the bed!" She was constantly poking around in the fire and never once paid me any attention.

Finally after several hours of enjoying our nice campfire, we retired to bed. My wife was sick. She had breathed in too much smoke. She was sick to her stomach and had a severe headache. She threw up several times that night. We were in our first 'pop up' and the bathroom was across the street!   She was really, really sick! No matter how many times I told her, "I told you not to play in that fire," she wouldn't feel better. It was a long night of camping for my wife that night! She did learn a lesson about campfires though.

My wife doesn't poke around in the fires as much as she did, but she still likes to! She felt a lot better the next morning and you might think that she would not ever want to see another fire, but there is something.....a wonderful feeling.....a peace that falls on you when sitting around a campfire. We have spent many wonderful hours; have met many new friends and swapped lots and lots of stories around campfires.

It's a lot of trouble to haul around bundles of fire wood and it can be really expensive if you opt to buy fire wood when you get where you are going. We bought a small twelve inch grill for $3.95 at a dollar discount store and found some 'fire logs' on sale at K-Mart. (Wal Mart is just as good) Now for those that don't know what a fire log is, it is a log that is made out of saw dust and wax and no telling what else, but any way, you can buy them for about a buck apiece and even cheaper if you hit a sale. They are designed to burn in home fire places, but work wonderfully well as campfire logs. The logs are sealed in a paper covering. We usually haul around at least five or six with us. They stack really well and don't leave a mess like hauling around old logs, etc. do. You just light the ends of the paper with a match and in a few minutes you have a really nice campfire that will burn for two to three hours with no fuss and the fire logs put out only a fraction of the smoke a wood fire sometimes does. I also must tell you that the fire logs usually only put out a fraction of the heat that wood fires do. I usually douse my log with charcoal lighter fluid and it gets going a lot faster. If you let the log burn completely out, it leaves very little ash and therefore hardly no mess to clean up!

If you have never had the pleasure of relaxed conversation with your family and friends while sitting around a campfire, you have missed one of the great things in life. Don't get cheated!

Have the campfire experience at the first opportunity! It will be an experience you will want to repeat often.

Camping Tip: Check with the campground or RV Park on what the rules are for campfires, Sometimes permission to build a campfire will depend upon the local weather conditions. Remember that fires should be attended at all times and make sure the fire is COMPLETELY OUT before going to bed or leaving the site.

PLEASE: Don't throw aluminum cans or tin cans into the fire. Believe me they won't burn and the next camper to use the site doesn't want to see your garbage in his fire ring.

We burn fire logs on a small Bar B Q grill. The grill keeps the fire off the ground and the ashes fall into the grill for easy clean up.

Chapter 12: Why an RV?

One of the reasons we decided to buy our first camper was **vacation money**...we didn't have any! You ask, "How can buying an R.V. solve a vacation money problem?" Well, we sat down and tried to figure out just how we could go on a vacation. We had never taken a vacation. My Mom and Dad had taken vacations and when we saw the photos and heard the stories, we were ready to go. We just didn't have the means to go. I was working as a police officer and I surely was not making an abundance of money. In fact I was just making enough money to get by...barely.

My Dad had purchased a 'Pop Up' (tent trailer) camper and he couldn't say enough good things about camping. One of the things he said was how inexpensive campground spaces were in relation to hotel or motel rooms. (You could camp at a KOA campground for about $4.00 a night back then. *(Yes, it was a long, long time ago in a galaxy far, far away!!!)* A light went off in my head! We could afford to go **'IF'** we could get an RV without a great big investment and a large monthly note.

I started looking around for a used "Pop Up" and it wasn't long before I answered a newspaper ad and purchased a Star Craft trailer for $600.00.

Now we could afford to go on vacations and weekend trips if we really watched our money and stuck to a stiff budget. We figured that we had to eat any way and so we always brought a lot of food with us. *(It took us a while to figure out there were grocery stores in other places besides the town where we lived.)* With the trailer, which had a stove and sink, etc., we could virtually cut out restaurant bills and paying campground fees was only a fraction of the cost of hotel rooms.

Camping With Kids

Without that first "Pop Up' trailer we would have missed out on many wonderful trips. Our kids would have missed out on a good portion of what I call their **'real education'**. I believe that traveling can be an educational experience and we tried to make each vacation a learning experience for the children as well as for us. There were lots of times when my son would tell me about something they were studying in school and how he had told the teacher he had been there in person and had seen it for himself. He had "been there and done that" at an early age!

I was an avid Civil War nut and had taken the family to a lot of Civil War battlefields, old plantation homes and many other historical sites. We had roamed the hills of such places as Shilo, Tennessee, Vicksburg, Mississippi, Gettysburg, Pennsylvania, Fort Sumpter, South Carolina and Appomattox Court House, Virginia. We covered a lot of battlefields in Virginia and toured the old Confederate Capitol in Richmond.

We walked up and down the Capitol Mall in Washington, D.C. and toured the Smithsonian Institute museums. I wish you could have seen my son's eyes when he saw the dinosaur skeletons, or when he saw the airplanes hanging from the roof, or got to climb around on all those trains! We walked the halls of the White House, rode the elevator to the top of the Washington Monument and saw the changing of the guard at Arlington Cemetery.

We swam in the Atlantic Ocean and we swam in the Gulf of Mexico. We swam a lot in campground swimming pools too! We built campfires, ate picnic lunches and took a lot of pictures!

My youngest son learned to ride a bicycle on a campground.

We were camped in New Iberia, Louisiana at Belmont Campground. I had just taken the training wheels off his two-wheeler. He fell and fell and fell and fell, but each time he got up and tried again. I know he cussed out that bike, but he made sure I didn't hear him. He kept after it and then he just took off down the side of a small hill. He was riding!

I happened to be filming him with my old 8mm movie camera when he made his first ride! He held on to the handle bars so tightly that his knuckles were white and his hands hurt.

Each time we did these things was an experience to be remembered for a life time, but without our R.V. we would literally have had to stay home.

We went to Disney World when the Magic Kingdom was the only theme park there. We saw the place grow one theme park at a time. We stayed in Fort Wilderness at Walt Disney World when the trees were tiny, little sticks poking up out of the ground! *(We were in Fort Wilderness recently and commented on how big the trees were and how much they had grown.)*

I pulled up in a campground on the Tennessee-Alabama border and was setting up in our camp spot when my son came and told me that there were a bunch of cows next to our camp and that they only had hair on their front ends and no hair on their back ends. I told him to stay away from them, that they might have some sort of mange or other disease. I finished setting up and told him to show me the cows. We walked a little ways down a path that ended at a barbed wire fence. Grazing in the pasture were a few head of buffalo. He had never seen a buffalo, or bison, and it looked to him as though they only had hair on their front ends!

We fished for lobster in Maine, ate biscuits and gravy in the Smoky Mountains, rode down the Alpine Slide in Chattanooga, Tennessee, snorkeled for shells in Panama City, Florida and swatted mosquitoes in the swamps of Louisiana. We rode the Maid of the Mist to the base of Niagara Falls, rode a boat on the underground lake in the Lost Sea Caverns, saw the giant sculpture at Stone Mountain, Georgia, dug for diamonds in Arkansas, went to Branson, Missouri when they had only one show, went to Dollywood when it was called Silver Dollar City and we did all this WITH THE KIDS!!!!!

For the first time in our lives, we had the means to travel the country and we didn't have to be millionaires. We didn't eat in the finest restaurants. We didn't stay in the five star hotels. We weren't pampered and waited on, but we weren't stuck at home either!

We had a ball! We would sit around those campfires and wonder what the rich people were doing! If camping would not have been so affordable, we would have loved it any way. Each time we hooked up and headed down the road we got excited! We were on a great adventure! We couldn't wait to see what was around the next curve. We got used to the question being asked from the back seat, "Are we there yet?"

One time when we were on our way back home from a camping trip on Dolphin Island, Alabama, I noticed that the gas gauge was leaning toward the empty mark. I had a certain gas credit card I wanted to use and so I passed exit after exit on I-10 knowing in my heart after passing each one that I should have stopped and gassed up, but I hadn't seen the right kind of station. Finally, I decided to pull off and get gas. The engine started to sputter and cough and the car just stopped right on the exit ramp. I got out and I won't tell you what I had to say about it, but it was my fault and that made it worse! I went back to our Song Bird trailer that we were towing and had to dump a whole gallon of red Cool Aid on the ground so I could use the plastic jug for a gas can. I was only about a quarter of a mile from the station. I rinsed out the Cool Aid jug and filled it up with a gallon of gas and walked back to the car. I put the gas in the tank and the car still would not start. I took the breather off the carburetor and poured the few drops of gas that was still in the jug down into its' mouth. The engine started right up and I drove on down to the station and finished filling the tank with gas. Boy did I hear about that from my wife and the kids, especially my youngest one! It was just another memory to add to our list of adventures.

Camping Tip: PLEASE! Check the gas gage and don't get hard headed about where to gas up like I did. Since this experience we have spent a lot of time RVing out west and up into Canada. In some places it pays to fill up the gas tank when you have a chance to fill up, whether you think you need it or not. We have been to numerous places where the gas stations might be 100 miles apart.

The kids are all grown now and out on their own, but they still like to meet Mom and Dad and spend time camping. I believe that camping can get "in your blood" and you can't ever get it out. I know it's in me and I don't want it to get out! I still get excited when it's time to head down the road. I guess I always will.

A South Dakota tailgate party

Camped next to a big lake in Arkansas.

Camping with Mom and June on the Gulf Coast.

Chapter 13: Dreams Can Come True

I guess we started dreaming about "full timing" right after our very first vacation. For those of you that don't know what "full timing" means, it's when you give away or sell everything you have, house, furniture, appliances, excess clothing and all the treasures (or junk) you have collected after years of living in a regular house, move into your RV and drive off without looking back!

There was wander lust in us and every time we hit the road we never wanted to turn around and go back. I used to tell people that I brought a gun with me on every trip so when it was time to return home, I would give the gun to my wife and she would force me at gun point to drive back to our home town! I liked traveling so much that one day when she told me to turn around and go home, I told her to go ahead and shoot!

Well, it really wasn't that bad, but we really, really liked to travel. Then I had a thought planted in my head.

Location: Tropical Palms Camp Resort. Kissimmee, Florida

I was camped next to an elderly man and his wife, who were staying in a motor home. He came out and started talking to me. (Maybe I came out and started talking to him, because I don't know any strangers, I just don't know every one's name!) So, he started telling me that he and his wife had been on the road, camping, for TWENTY YEARS!!!!!

Needless to say I had about three thousand four hundred and seventy six questions that I wanted to ask him. He told me that he had retired and decided to 'sell out' and just go on a trip until he got tired of traveling. He was still on the road having a great time after twenty years. He had worn out three motor homes and he needed a new one. He told me that he was going to have to stop traveling, because his wife was having some physical problems and that his eye sight was failing. He couldn't see to drive as well as he used to. I detected a tear in his eye when he told me that he was going to have to quit traveling.

He told me things that he and his wife had seen and done together, places they had visited and people they had met. It was a great story and I was inspired. I don't remember his name or the brand name of rig he was driving, other than he was in a motor home. I don't even know if he is still alive, (I met him around 1988 and he must have been at least seventy years old then) but he lit a fire in me. For the first time in my life I realized that *IT WAS POSSIBLE TO GO ON A VACATION.... AND JUST KEEP ON GOING!!!!!*

The wheels began to turn in my head and it wasn't long before my wife and I were talking about becoming 'full timers'. That name did have a certain ring about it. I told some of the guys I worked with about full timing and of course they thought I was crazy. I believe that people get settled into a life style of getting up and going to work and then going home and then going to work and waiting for the weekends, or for their days off so they can just lay around the house and watch TV. I tried that and I didn't like it. To me it was not living... just existing. I wanted some action! I wanted to see new places, meet new people, eat new foods and see how other people lived. In short, I didn't want to stay home, I wanted to go out and play! I wanted to enjoy life, not just endure it and as much as we liked camping and traveling.... well, why not?

My wife and I began to talk to other full timers that we ran across in campgrounds. We read several magazine articles and we even found a book with all kinds of information about full timing. We knew what we wanted to do. We wanted to become full timers, but we knew we would have to have a plan.

Of course I mean a financial plan. Being a police officer, I was in a retirement system, but to take off and travel and expect to live on a pension meant that we couldn't be tied down with a lot of monthly bills. Really, we needed to get rid of **ALL** of our monthly bills. We thought about this and thought about this and finally came up with our plan of action. If we paid off as many bills as we could and with the income from the police pension when I retired, we could do it. The key was to keep our monthly bills to a minimum, so we made a timetable for our departure into the world of full timing...three years. This gave us time to pay off notes, start unloading all the treasures and junk we had accumulated over the years and acquire our retirement date.

At first, three years seemed like a lifetime. I wanted to go full timing and I wanted to go NOW! The three year schedule would be best for us and we both knew it. I was the Chief of Police in my home town at the time and I had good vacation benefits and we could go on several one to three week vacations per year, so this would do us until our financial plan was completed.

The first thing we did was to start having yard sales. (Some people call them garage sales, but we didn't have a garage. My Grandfather always called them garbage sales.) We started looking around the house for the things we hadn't used in ten years and we started finding some things we hadn't even seen in ten years. We sold them. I wanted to sell our lawn mower and trimmers right off, but my wife insisted that we would need to use them over the next three years. I pled my case, but, my argument fell on deaf ears so I kept the lawn equipment. She even made me keep the paint brushes and rollers!

We would have a big yard sale and as soon as it was over with, my wife would start gathering up our next batch of stuff. When she had accumulated enough treasure, another yard sale would ensue. We made some money (it is usually easy to sell perfectly good things for ten cents on a dollar) and paid bills. What did we sell? We started with the china closet. My wife had a lot of plates and other 'untouchables' in the china closet and they went in the first yard sale. Did she miss her treasures? Probably, but she didn't miss having to continually dust them any more!

We sold clothes, we sold books, we sold tapes (we didn't have any CD's then) we sold shoes and Christmas decorations. We found out that Christmas decorations will sell fast no matter what time of the year it is. I guess people want to be in the Christmas spirit even in July. We sold the bed out of the spare bed room, the pictures off the walls, anything that was considered not a basic necessity for living in the house, we sold.

This went on from time to time throughout that three year period. We had one yard sale after another. I was so tired of hauling things out to the front yard and when we were finished, hauling what did not sell back into the house.

We found out that as time went on and our retirement day drew imminent, that those treasures we had been hoarding up for all those years really didn't seem as important as they used to. We came to learn that they were just things...you know just... 'stuff'. We had to make a decision when we decided that we wanted to become full timers. If we wanted to keep our personal treasures, all the 'stuff' that we had been accumulating over the years, then we had to keep the house. Keeping a house would be more monthly expenses. Not counting any house payments, there is insurance, light bill, water bill etc. Someone would have to be hired to do the lawn. (In south Louisiana if you don't cut your lawn about twice a week in the summer time you will not be able to find your house.) If you don't live in the house and the house is sitting there unoccupied a lot of insurance companies won't cover you and an unoccupied house deteriorates rapidly. I also knew that if we would keep a house, then we would constantly be going back to check on it and that was the same as having to go home just when the vacation was getting good.

We went on a vacation to the Smoky Mountains in Tennessee in June of 1991. We had a great time doing all of the mountain things like hiking, picnicking, going to Dollywood, eating all those biscuits and gravy and just enjoying the beautiful scenery. When we returned home, I had barely backed our Coachmen travel trailer into our driveway when the telephone started to ring in the house. My wife answered it and came outside where I was unhooking the rig and told me that someone had just called and wanted to buy our stove. They had heard that we were 'selling out' and they wanted the stove. I thought we still needed a stove, but my wife for some strange reason, didn't want to keep it. We thought about it for a few minutes. This was in June and I wasn't scheduled to retire until October. Finally I said, "We had better sell it if someone wants to buy it." I didn't want to wait until the day of retirement and get stuck holding a lot of appliances and furniture. I had my wife call the person back and we sold the stove. The word seemed to spread very quickly that what we had was up for grabs. In the next few weeks the washer and dryer were sold, then the refrigerator and the freezer, the living room furniture, the dining room furniture, the bed room furniture. We even sold the satellite dish. **_Finally I got to sell the lawn mower!!!!!_**

We took our things that we couldn't seem to part with, our old photos, home video tapes, Bibles and cards and things that the children had made for us when they were little and other mementos and carefully packed them away in card board boxes and stored them in my mother's attic.

A friend of mine came over and we spent an entire day adding shelving to the cabinets in our Coachmen travel trailer. This almost doubled our storage space. We took our clothes, pots and pans, and other **necessities** (like the TV and the VCR) and put them in our trailer. This is when we really started finding out that storage space...any storage space, was a precious commodity!

We had inherited a black, Chinese Chow dog. My youngest son's girl friend had given him the dog for a birthday present. My son had since moved to Lafayette, Louisiana where he had taken a job as a radio D. J. The girl friend was gone, my son was gone, but the dog was still there. I liked the dog.... OK, I loved the dog, but we had decided that we were not going to be tied down to a pet when we were traveling. Now I know that a lot of folks travel with pets and I'm glad that they are doing what they want to do and I have nothing against this, but I figured that if we were off touring Disney World, or where ever, that I wouldn't want to have to leave and go back to the RV because the dog needed to be let out. We didn't want to be on anybody's schedule except our own and we certainly didn't want to be on a dog's schedule.

I looked for a good family to give the dog to. He was pure bred and we had all the papers on him. Finally just a few days before we moved into the trailer I found a man with a nice, fenced in yard, a wife that liked dogs and two little girls that couldn't wait to love on that dog. We gave "Baby Bear" away. I was glad, on the one hand, that the dog had a good home, but on the other hand, I sort of went into mourning, as if a family member had died. Parting with friends is not easy, even if the friend is a black, fifty pound dog.

What Have We Done?

We were out of the house and living in our Coachmen travel trailer that was parked on our driveway. We had literally sold out. All of the furniture was gone. All of our appliances were sold and carted off. We were staying on the driveway in front of a big, empty house. Whatever was left in the house that didn't sell, we threw out in the trash.

When we discussed how we were going to be full timers we had set a schedule to be moved into the RV around September 1st and my retirement date was set for October 1st and here we were 'camped out' on our driveway and it was July 20th!

We made all of our arrangements to be free from the house and on July 24, 1991 we hooked the trailer up to the hitch on our Chevrolet Suburban and pulled the rig to our new temporary home at the Lake End Park Campground, located on the edge of Morgan City about two miles from our house.

We had very mixed emotions. We were glad and happy to see our dreams starting to come true...and at the same time it was a great emotional upheaval to leave our home of over twenty years. We had raised our children in that house. We were living there when I graduated from college. I had spent almost all of the years of my police career there. That house was the site of much happiness, many pleasant memories and now we were just going to pull away and leave it!

I remember standing in my driveway with the rig hooked up to the Suburban. My wife was sitting on the passenger side of the front seat, waiting to leave. I had been in the house checking around for the twentieth time, making sure we hadn't forgotten anything, or left anything. I walked outside and looked back at the house and then I looked at the trailer and the Suburban. For a few moments a feeling of great grief overwhelmed me. WHAT HAD WE DONE? We had gotten rid of the very things that most people spend their lives trying to accumulate. We had sold or given away everything that most people rely on and trust in as their 'security'. What in the world had we done? Had we made a very big mistake? Were we really as crazy as some of our friends had said we were? If this was the beginning of a great adventure, why did it feel like everything had come to an end? Everything that most people work for all their lives was gone. Our children were gone. The house belonged to someone else. What ever we thought was valuable enough to keep was stored in someone else's attic. I walked over to the Suburban, got in and drove off. It sure was a quiet ride in that Suburban that day.

Once we got to the campground and got the rig set up we were in better spirits. The dream had truly started! The dream was coming true! A little ahead of schedule, perhaps, but our adventure had started! *Even if we had only gone two miles!*

Camping Tip: As much as I enjoy full timing, I realize that this lifestyle is not for everyone. If you plan on doing this you need to be really sure about it, *before* you launch off into the world of being a modern day Gypsy. Find out all you can by reading magazine articles and books on the subject. Get your RV and travel to as many campground and RV resort as you can, so you can get a feel for what is in store for you. Talk to the full timers (you can usually find them on just about every RV park) that you encounter while camping. They can give you information from their experiences that you can learn of from no other source.

You have to take into account the wishes of your spouse and other family members. My wife and I couldn't wait to get on the road ... and ... we still love heading out to new adventures. Remember, we planned this and thought about this and studied this for a long time before we moved out on the road full time.

Take your time and don't rush into anything. Plan carefully and you can keep the "surprises" to a minimum. Don't get upset if anyone tell you that to go 'full timing' is crazy!

Our new Bounder Motor Home

Our motor home in an RV park in California

Home Sweet Home in Anchorage

Chapter 14: The Transition

We were now full fledged "full timers". We were living in a RV travel trailer in a RV park. We pulled into our camping spot and as I attempted to unhitch, the electric jack broke again! We were off to a great start. I had kept the hand crank jack in a compartment on the side of the trailer and in just a few minutes I had it changed out and the trailer leveled and set up. We were on site E-3 in the Lake End Park and would be there for the next two months.

We discovered that the refrigerator was not working. Wonderful! After checking everything I knew how to check, I finally had to call a repairman. The fridge would work on propane gas, but not on electric. The repairman showed up and gave me a $30.00 lesson on how to check the electric heating coil. I asked a lot of questions about how to change the coil and when I learned that it was not difficult I ordered the part and told him to call me when it came in. (I was still working and I had my police cell phone.) The heating coil came in a few days later and I changed it myself after paying $52.80 for the part. The refrigerator worked fine and was still working fine when we traded the trailer in. The repairman told me it was not good to turn the refrigerator off when the trailer was not in use. Condensation could form in the coil and that would cause the wires to rust and corrode. Not knowing any better, we had always cleaned the refrigerator and turned it off when it was stored on our driveway.

Camping Tip: When you return home from an outing, plug in your RV and leave the refrigerator on. This will prevent condensation from forming in the heating coils, which will cause the coil wires to rust and the refrigerator not to work properly.

We were still a little torn between giving up the house and starting our dream of being 'professional' tourists. When we realized the six hundred plus dollars a month we were going to save by not having an electric bill or house payment, or telephone bill etc., we did feel a lot better.

My youngest son, Randy Jr., came in from Lafayette, Louisiana to visit us. I could see that our getting out of the house had had an emotional impact on him. All of a sudden there were strange people living in the house that he had spent his entire life living in. I know that giving up the dog bothered him, although he was living in another town and didn't see the dog that often. I guess that although a person leaves home to find his own place in life, that there is that sense of security knowing that good ole' Mom and Dad are right there at home with the dog and you can call or visit when ever the need arises. And now here were Mom and Dad about to turn into Nomads wondering around the country.

I was still getting up every morning and going to work. Not exactly the great adventure I had in my mind when I envisioned being a full timer. I have to admit, there was still a sense of excitement about me. I looked forward to getting off work and going to the campground. My retirement date was getting closer day by day.

We spent a lot of time rearranging our belongings. We would move things around and then, maybe in a few days, move the same things around again until finally we had things stored by size and in relation to how often we used them. We ended up with more room for storage than we had first anticipated. Not great, giant, empty, caverns of storage space, but more than we thought we would have. One thing is true, if you are full timing, there is never enough storage space in your RV.

The Lake End Park is situated right on a big lake. *(Of course)* After work I would walk down to the boat ramp and fish for bass. Almost every day I caught a few fish and even brought some fish home for my wife to clean. (She really likes to clean fish!) We were enjoying the good life and eating fish too.

We had a lot of visitors during our stay at the park. Everyone was curious as to how we could move out of a perfectly good house and move into a twenty-eight foot travel trailer and be happy about it. There were one or two people jealous of us and wishing they could drop everything and go with us. Most of them just shook their heads and asked a lot of questions like, "What will you do when you have seen everything?" Or "What will you do if you decide to quit traveling?" or "What will happen if you decide you don't like traveling and want to come home?" Some people acted as if there was no turning back after we left and went on the road. Could they possibly believe that we could...**see everything!** Or that if we decided to quit traveling that we couldn't just...**stop traveling!** If we did want to return to our hometown, or any other town, couldn't we just...**buy another house?** Some people have some strange ideas or either they don't think a lot before they ask questions. I do know that the idea of traveling around without a permanent home to return to baffles some people. It didn't baffle us, however, and we could hardly wait for the retirement to start. We had "home" hooked up to our back bumper!

I was wearing a coat and tie to work every day and I had a lot of them. They were hung around the trailer taking up a lot of room, but I needed them for work. As I approached the final days of my employment I decided to get rid of all those coats and ties. They were getting pretty well worn, because I had held off buying new ones. I didn't foresee needing any sport coats, ties or suits in my full timing adventures. Each evening when I got off work I would drive to the campsite and park the car in the front of the trailer. When I got out of the car, I would take my coat, tie and shirt off and walk across the street to the trash bin and throw them in! I'll bet my camping neighbors must have thought we were filthy rich. "That guy doesn't worry about his dry cleaning bills. He just wears his coats and ties and when he's finished, he just throws them away!"

On September 20, 1991, I put in my last day with the Police Department. I was on vacation and compensatory time until my official retirement date of October 1. Although we had been anxiously waiting for my retirement date, it was still hard to believe that I didn't have to get up and go to work anymore. There would be no constant ringing of the telephone. (We didn't even have a telephone now!) I didn't have to be continually thinking about all of the employees that worked under me or, the one hundred plus prisoners that were under my care in the jail. I was truly free to do what I wanted to do and I didn't have to answer to anyone! (Except my wife, of course)

I took the Suburban into the shop to have the transmission serviced and while the truck was on the rack the mechanic called me over and pointed out to me that the radiator was leaking and needed attention. I had to have the radiator pulled and fixed and after it was all replaced and looked as good as new were ready to go.

On our last night in the Lake End Park, a big south Louisiana thunderstorm broke upon us early in the morning. It rained and rained, the lightning flashed and the thunder rolled. Since this is a common occurrence in Louisiana, we were still in bed, listening to the rain pounding on the roof, when I heard a horrible, metal twisting, dragging, scrapping sound. I remembered that the awning was still out! I jumped out of bed and ran to the door (about two steps) and lifted the shade and looked out. All I could see was the awning hanging in front of the door. **'CATASTROPHE!!! BIG MONEY TO FIX THIS!!!'** I thought, as I looked out into the storm.

I hurriedly dressed, although I don't know why, since any damage that was done to the awning was already done. I could hardly open the door to get out. The awning material was draped down in front of the door and it was full of water. I emptied the water and stood around outside getting wet, because it was still raining. I must have looked like one of those guys in the disaster movies, standing out there all wet in the wind and rain. After emptying all the water, I was able to stretch the awning out and check the damage. The two supports that attach to the roof of the camper and adjust out to keep the awning taunt were bent. I couldn't see any other damage. I was able to partially roll the awning up and I left it like that and retired back inside the trailer to dry out, drink coffee and worry about the awning damage until the rain stopped.

Once the rain stopped I was back outside with my wife, checking the damage. I rolled the awning back out and got my ladder (all full timers have a ladder) and got up and removed the two bent braces. It had rained so hard that the water couldn't run off the awning fast enough, even though one end of the awning was about six inches lower than the other end. Once the water started forming a "belly" in the vinyl material, more and more water accumulated until it forced those braces to give. I had a seventeen-foot awning with no center support and that didn't help any, although I had been assured by the RV dealer that they only put center supports on awnings of over eighteen feet in length. Missed it by one!

I took those braces, which were made of aluminum, and found a picnic table that had the table boards spaced about an inch and a half apart. I put in a brace and pulled and pulled until it was straight. Well, it was almost straight and you couldn't tell it was bent unless you really looked at it closely. I did the same thing with the other one and reinstalled them on the awning. The awning worked as well as it always did, almost. After that I never left the awning out when we left the rig or retired for the night. Since then I have seen several awnings blown over their camper's roofs by winds, and bent all out of shape by rain. I just don't take any chances. I roll the awning up when I'm not around or before we go to bed.

Camping Tip: It is a good idea when leaving the RV or retiring for the night to roll up your awning. I have seen thunderstorms come up without warning and wreak havoc on RV awnings on more than one occasion. A few minutes to roll the awning safely up could save a big repair or replacement bill. Now you can purchase an electric awning that rolls out and rolls in with the touch of a button. I don't have one yet, but my mouth waters whenever I see one!

Having put everything back together we hooked up and went to Five Star Resort in Pass Christian, Mississippi where we have a camping membership. We were finally on our great adventure. We had made it out of town. We were full timing and we were even in another state!

But, we weren't through with 'home' yet. We had to go back to Morgan City to get some banking business straight. We went back on the 30th of September. We took care of our business and then stayed at my mother's house having left our trailer in Mississippi.

There is a big light in my mother's yard that shines right into the front bedroom where my wife and I were staying. The mattress was a lot harder than the one we were used to sleeping on in the camper. We tossed and turned and tossed some more. Mother has a big grandfather clock in her living room. Every fifteen minutes it chimed *loudly* announcing that we were not sleeping! Neither of us slept at all that night. Dawn was a welcomed sight to both of us. We got up and drank a lot of coffee and headed back to Five Star Resort. I drove up and parked at the camper and we got out. I unlocked the door and we went inside. I felt this great peace come over me. I knew my wife, June, felt it too and we both commented on it. **WE WERE HOME!** Our Coachmen travel trailer had indeed become our home. We were relaxed there and comfortable. We were at ease. We knew that we were where we were supposed to be.

Now important decisions had to be made. There were important questions to be answered. Where were we going? How long did we think we should stay? Which direction should we head first? We were free! Free to come and go as we wanted. We weren't on any schedule! We could go anywhere and stay as long as we wanted to!

We had enjoyed our two months of camping and working, but now the working part was over. We had embarked on a new profession....we were *'professional'* tourists! Our short transition period was over. We had successfully made the switch from house living to travel trailer living and we liked it! Our outlook was bright! Our future held high adventure! We were off to see the world and to experience things, small and great! We were living the great American dream....**we were on our never ending vacation!!!!!**

Chapter 15: Life on the Road
How Do I Get My Mail?

Living on the road can bring some problems that you don't experience when living in one permanent location. For instance, usually every day I went to our local post office in Morgan City and got our mail. We had a post office box for over twenty years. Getting your mail is not something that usually takes a lot of thought. Either the mail person brings the mail to your house, office or post office box and you just pick it up. When on the road in different places all the time, receiving mail can be a problem.

Mail can be sent, addressed to you at General Delivery, to the post office in any town. This seems simple enough and it is, but being in strange places all the time, the big question we hear being asked around the campground is: "Where is Wal Mart?" and then the second question is, "Where is the post office?" The knowledge of the location of these two places seems to be of concern to almost every traveler that spends a lot of time on the road. Remember, being in towns and cities you have never visited means that you don't know where anything is! Some city maps show the location of post offices and some don't.

Another thing we found out is that all post offices do not accept General Delivery mail. If you are in a large city, usually the General Delivery mail is accepted only at the main post office. On several occasions we have cheerfully gone into a post office to retrieve our mail, only to be told that the General Delivery mail was at another post office all the way across town.

Usually the people working at the campground can tell you where to have your mail sent. Some campgrounds will not accept visitor mail, so you should check with them before you have your mail shipped on ahead of you. Another thing to remember is that if the campground does accept mail, it will probably take you an extra day to have the mail delivered to the campground instead of picking it up at the Post Office.

In this modern day of Priority Mail, with two to three day delivery, getting mail is not the problem it once was. Of course there are other mail services, like Fed-X and UPS, which can have your mail in your hands overnight, if you want to pay the extra money.

Right before we started full timing, I had our address changed over to my Mother's Post Office box address. She gathers up all the mail and we call and tell her where to ship it. This has worked out great for us and I hope it's not too great an inconvenience for my Mother.

If you don't have a family member, or friend, that is willing to take on the task of gathering up your mail to be forwarded to you, then there are several service companies that will do this for you for a fee. Mail Box, Etc., the UPS Store and some other companies will perform this service for a nominal charge. You have to rent one of their mail boxes and have your mail sent there and the company will forward your mail to you where ever you tell them to send it.

Banking on the Road

Banking really caused us a problem when we first hit the road. When you are out of state your checkbook is generally not worth the paper the checks are printed on. There are several places, however, that will accept your check. Wal Mart will take your check for the amount of purchase and we have made purchases by check with them all over the USA. Another place that will usually cash your check is gambling casinos. I know that they expect you to cash a check and then leave the money in their slot machines, but they will usually cash checks with not a lot of problems. Be sure to have proper ID.

Now in the day of the ATM card, getting money while on the road is no longer a problem. ATM machines are everywhere and if your card is connected to one of the big networks, such as Cirrus or Plus, you can virtually have access to your money anytime and in almost any place.

You can get Debit Cards issued from your bank. A Debit Card looks like a Visa or MasterCard, but when you use it the money is withdrawn directly from your checking account. In effect you **CAN** write checks in any place that accepts credit cards, if you use one of these Debit Cards. A Debit Card and Direct Deposit to your bank account and you are in business.

We had not been full timing very long, when we stopped in Unadilla, Georgia. We needed some cash and I had an ATM card. I spotted a nice looking bank on the main street of the business district. The bank had several drive up banking stalls and looked really modern, so I pulled into the parking lot. I didn't see any ATM machines, so I got out of my Suburban and went into the bank. We had learned that some banks have their ATMs inside. I got into the lobby and I still didn't see any machine. I walked up to the girl at the counter and asked her where the ATM machine was. She replied to me that she didn't know what an ATM was. I tried to explain that it was a bank machine where you could put in your card and you could get money out of your checking or savings account. She said, "Yea, sure!"

I really did need some cash. I got out my map and was looking for a larger town, where perhaps, ATM machines were not something out of a science fiction movie, when I noticed that there was an Air Force base about twenty-five miles north. I drove up there and sure enough they knew what an ATM machine was and I got some money.

Three times, however, my wife and I have gone up to an ATM machine, put the card in and requested that the machine give us $300.00. The machine whirred and clanked and gave us a receipt showing that we had received $300.00, but no money came out!

The first time this happened to us, we were **greatly** distressed! Really I wanted to take a sledge hammer to that machine and make it **give me my money!** (Of course this happened at night when banks are closed, you can't get in touch with anyone that is a real person on the telephone and then you can think about your $300.00 that you didn't get out of the machine all night.)

I called my home bank the next day and they assured me that the error would straighten itself out and that it would take about seven working days. It did.

Once in a bank in Palmer, Alaska, the machine gave us the receipt and no money, but the bank was open for business. We went in and advised the really nice lady that was working behind the counter, what had happened. She went and checked the machine and came back and told us that the machine had indeed malfunctioned and that it would all be corrected in about seven working days! She was nice enough to cash a personal check for us, so we would have some cash. Most ATM cards have daily limits on how much money you can withdraw. Of course, once the ATM thinks it has given you your money, even if it really hasn't, you can't go to another machine to get your cash if you have tried to draw out your limit! No need to worry! It will all be corrected in seven working days!

Aside from the three times this has happened to us, the ATM Check Card is the best thing going and we couldn't get along without one now.

We were in Dodge City, Kansas in 1992 and we couldn't find an ATM that would accept our brand of ATM card. Back then there were several companies or banks that had ATM cards, but you had to find an ATM machine that was affiliated with that particular bank for it to work. It was a good thing that we had gas credit cards and a Visa charge card or I would probably be writing this from Dodge City! Now with all the big ATM networks that provide service all over the world, this is no longer the big problem that it once was.

In 1992, I pulled into Tok, Alaska and stopped at the tourist information center. We saw the exhibits and some of the tourist films they were showing. On my way out I asked one of the men working at the information center where the nearest ATM machine was. He told me, "Go out of the parking lot and take a right on the Alaska Highway. Then follow the highway for about 100 miles. The ATM is in Delta Junction." He smiled a great big smile and I knew I had made his day. (There is an ATM in Tok now.)

Telephones and Other Types of Communication

We got a cell phone to take along with us so if anyone wanted to find us they could just call. This was back when the cell phone craze was just starting. The problem with a cell phone back then was that when someone called you…**YOU PAID!**

We advised everyone that the number was just in case of an emergency, but every now and then someone would just get lonesome and call anyway. If the cell phone was not used in your "home" area (the place where you bought it) then you would have to pay what is called "Roaming" charges. This means that once your telephone goes on "Roam" you were at the mercy of whatever cell phone company was handling the calls in the area you were traveling in. For instance we were camped in Tulsa, Oklahoma. We went to town grocery shopping and I left the cell phone at the RV. I forgot to turn it off when we left. When we returned the cell phone gave me the message that we had missed one call. The telephone I had at the time didn't tell who called, just that you missed a call. When I got my bill I had been charged $3.30 for that missed call. I called my cellular company and complained, but to no avail. I had to pay it any way. Since our cell phone stayed on "Roam" all the time, it would have been nice to have a pre set cost so you could anticipate the monthly bill total. We canceled our cell phone contract back then because of the high cost of "Roaming" all the time.

Since then the cell phone companies have come out with all types of no roaming and no long distance charges, so we have another one. So far it has worked wonderfully well and we know in advance how much the bill is going to be every month. Cell phones have become a necessity now days and we wouldn't want to get on the road without one.

Another option to consider is having a **"Beeper"**. You can receive messages without receiving the phone call. There are several companies that offer nation wide beeper service. These beepers will work in most populated areas of the nation and you will have a way for people to get in touch with you for a nominal fee. Once you get a message you can call back at your leisure or not call back at your leisure, *(if you know what I mean.)*

For several years we had a **voice mail** service, which was the only way anyone could find us. It worked well, but each day or two we had to find a telephone and then call to see if anyone was trying to get in touch with us. This service worked well, but we still felt isolated. Even when we checked in with the message center and found out that there were no messages, the thought that someone might be trying to find us just a few minutes after our messages were checked, went through our minds.

We did find one thing that has served us very well in our travels. **E-Mail!** We bought an e-mail device at Quartzsite, Arizona that allows us to send and receive e-mail using any telephone. It works great with pay telephones also. The devise is small, can be carried in your pocket and runs off AA batteries. It has a small built in keyboard like a typewriter and a liquid crystal screen to read what you have typed and the messages sent to you.

The device cost about $100.00 and around $100.00 for a year of unlimited service with a company called Pocket Mail. We type messages to our family and friends who have computers and then find the nearest phone and dial an 800 number. The devise is placed against the earpiece and the speaker on the telephone handset and a button is pushed on the back of the e-mail unit and then it sends and receives our e-mail in a matter of seconds. We have used it all over the US and Canada and find it works very satisfactory. Paying the fee by the year does away with any monthly bills. We love it and we type messages (our Travel Log Updates) and send them to several people at one time, rather than type a lot of different letters.

The e-mail devise also serves as our address book. We store names and addresses and telephone number, as well as e-mail addresses, birthdays, notes and I even record when I need to change the oil in our vehicles.

Lots of RV parks have computer hook ups and if you have a laptop you can plug it in and receive and send e-mail. I understand that if you have the proper satellite equipment that you can hook the computer up to it and send and receive your e-mail. (I don't have this type of equipment **yet**, but it sure seems like a great idea!)

When all is considered, for fast, two way communications, the cell phone is the way to go. When someone needs to find you, they simply call you on the telephone. When you want to find someone, you simply call them on the telephone. Most cell phones will tell you when you missed a call, who called and at what time and most of them come with built in voice mail. *The cell phone can be worth its weight in gold if you break down on the road and need to call for assistance!*

Medical Help

I have heard several people tell me that they can't travel because they have to stay close to their doctor. Some of these people had some on going physical problems, but some of them didn't. I believe that some people have a fear of leaving the every day familiar things and going off to places where nothing is familiar. No matter how much you talk to these people, you are not going to convince them, that there is life in other places, that there are grocery stores in other towns, that you can buy clothes in other states, that almost every town has a doctor!

I got really sick in Bandera, Texas one time. My wife was sick too. We had the flu. I was out hooking up the electric and water, etc. for our travel trailer and I thought I was going to die right there. Then it dawned on me that I would have to feel a lot better than I was feeling to die! Now we were a long way from any of our family doctors. We needed help. I'm sure there are doctors in Bandera, but I went to the pay telephone and called a doctor in our hometown and told him our problems. He called a prescription for us into the drug store there in Bandera and we were much better in a few days.

My wife cut her fingers cleaning some salmon in Morgan's Landing State Park, just outside Soldotna, Alaska. (My wife really likes to clean fish!) I figured that her fingers couldn't be sewed up over the phone, so I put her in our Suburban and drove about five miles to town. I stopped in a little shopping center and went into a shop and asked the girl there for directions to a doctor's office. I told her the problem and she directed me to a doctor just up the street. I guess I could have brought her to the emergency room at the hospital, but I didn't know where the hospital was either. Besides, if you go to the emergency room you are fixing to pay **BIG** bucks for the same service you are going to get at a doctors office. (Of course in a medical emergency a hospital emergency room is the greatest place on earth!) We went into the doctor's office and he neatly stitched up her fingers…..and gave us a recipe for grilled salmon.

We have needed the services of a doctor on several occasions while out on the road and have always been able to find medical help nearby. Of course every time you walk into a doctor's office for your first visit, be ready to fill out mounds of paper work on your past medical history and on every other detail of your life over the past twenty years. I think that the doctors believe that filling out lots of papers must have a healing effect on the patient.

My wife became very ill and we took her to about a half dozen doctors who didn't seem to have a clue about what was wrong with her. After each new doctor we took the new prescription and had it filled and then she got worse! When I say that she was sick, I mean I was beginning to fear for her life--and she was too!

We were in a RV park on the Mississippi Gulf Coast and were watching a doctor on TV. He had a former patient on his show and she started telling about her symptoms. It could have been my wife telling her story on the TV. The Doctor was in Texas and as soon as the show was over I called the office, made an appointment with him and then packed up and drove the motor home non-stop to the town where the doctor was located.

Being "Full Timers" we didn't have to make a lot of plans for the trip. We just unhooked the electric wire, the water and sewer hoses, hooked up our tow car and took off!
Thanks to the Good Lord and that doctor (mostly the Good Lord!) my wife if fine now.

Time is Precious

A really great advantage of being out on the road is that you have time; time to stop and smell the roses, so to speak. We used to go to Disney World on vacation with the kids and buy five-day passes. We would always go in the summer time when the kids were out of school (and the crowds were the largest and it was the hottest!) and since I had to return in a matter of days to go to work, we embarked on a Disney marathon. We would be at one of the theme parks when they opened about 9:00 A.M. and stay until the parked closed. We would drag back to the RV about 2:00 A.M. After a few days of this we needed a vacation from our vacation. We wanted to get our money's worth (they don't give those Disney tickets away you know) so we stayed and stayed and saw and did as much as we could each day. We usually took a day off in the middle of the five-day marathon. We rested at the mall or some other restful retreat, like Sea World. When our vacation was over we were really beat!

Now, when we go to central Florida, after setting up the RV, we go to Disney World and purchase annual passes. With the annual pass, we feel free to come and go as we please. We don't feel the pressure to stay all day....**the pass is good for a year!** We go later and leave earlier. We can always go back tomorrow and it won't cost any more. And with annual passes you can park for FREE! Don't look for the price of the annual pass up on the ticket windows. It's not there, but ask and ye shall receive!

We've purchased annual passes over the years for Disney World, Universal Studios, Dollywood and we've bought some annual passes to the National Parks. We've saved a lot of money and feel the relief of being able to come and go as we please. A lot of the attractions also have special gates for annual pass holders so you don't have to spend so much time waiting in line just to get into the place.

Since we have been full timing, our trips to the "theme" parks have stretched out from days to weeks and some times even to months. We have a lot of time to leisurely see the parks, without being on a rush, rush, schedule. Next time you really want to see Disney World, go for two or three months instead of for a week. You will really enjoy yourself without the hectic go, go, go, go, of a short vacation! We've found out that this leisurely approach works in all kinds of places. It works at the beach; it works in the mountains, in the hills and in the valleys. *It really works when you're fishing!*

Home

Another place to visit when you are traveling is *"Home"*. Yes, you can go home after you have been full timing. You just take your RV and drive 'home.' You will probably find out that there is a campground right near your old hometown. If you announce your arrival in advance, I'm sure that there will be many offers to 'camp' in the driveways of friends and family. (Be sure to check on the local ordinances. In some places it is illegal to stay in your RV in the driveway.) We have spent time in the driveways of our relatives and have felt right at home, when we went 'home.' Of course, for us, home is where you park it!

On our first return visit to our hometown, I had a friend ask me all kinds of questions about full timing. He told me he wouldn't want to spend all of his time traveling. I knew this person and I knew that he really enjoyed going on vacations and taking trips. I tried to explain to him that full timing was just a never-ending vacation. He told me he didn't want to get up and drive all day long, every day. He had missed the whole point of full timing. The point being, that you have plenty of time, so that you don't have to spend every day driving up and down the highway. I don't enjoy driving all day and usually we don't. We like to travel about 150 to 200 miles and then stop. We have time and we aren't on a ridged schedule. We used to leave very early in the morning (5 or 6 AM) and drive fourteen hours to get to Disney World, or thirteen hours to get to the Smoky Mountains. The last time I drove from Disney World to our old home town took about five days…..and I was in a hurry!

I can't tell you how many tourist attractions we passed by while we headed to some particular attraction before we became full timers. We passed them up because we were pressed for time. We are not forced to do this any more. We have gotten up in the morning and started down the highway thinking we were going to travel several hundred miles. We started stopping at roadside tourist attractions and ended up driving about twenty-five miles in all. We love it!

Once in Mississippi, I ran across a full timing couple. They told me that they averaged about four or five hundred miles a day and they never stayed in one place longer than one or two nights! They eventually told me they were going to stop full timing because it wasn't fun. **It sure didn't sound like fun to me either!**

I met a couple on the side of the road in Nova Scotia, Canada, where we had pulled off to view a beautiful bridge and to take some pictures. They were from Houston, Texas and we quickly struck up a conversation. The man told me they had left Texas and were touring some of the Maritime Provinces of Canada. He had driven up through Maine and New Brunswick and was headed to Cape Breton Island in Nova Scotia. They were on a **SEVEN DAY VACATION!** I don't know if I would consider this to be a vacation. I think they were on a seven day driving marathon. I wouldn't want to go on a trip like that.....but if it was the only way I could go, knowing me, I'd probably go!

We are truly blessed to be able to take our time seeing all the things we only dreamed of seeing.

Another advantage we have realized by being on the 'endless vacation' is that the weather doesn't hamper us as it once did when we took short vacations. If we woke up and it was raining, or cold, or raining and cold, no matter how miserable, we just HAD to go where ever we were going. We had our mental schedule to follow and weather could not keep us from our appointed sightseeing! We had a limited number of days and always had more to do and see than time would permit, so no matter what the weather conditions, *we were tourists that would not be denied!*

For example, we were at Disney World in Florida one year, when a hurricane blew up out of the Gulf of Mexico. Being from Louisiana and having had a lot of experience with hurricanes, we anxiously watched the weather forecast on TV. It was a minimal hurricane and the weather forecast stated that by the time the storm system reached the Orlando area it would already be down graded to a tropical storm. Some friends had made the trip with us and after about ten seconds of discussion we decided to go to Epcot Center, in spite of the weather. (Up until this time Disney had never closed due to bad weather) We bought some of those fashionable, plastic, Disney, rain ponchos, with EPCOT CENTER printed on the front and spent the entire day wandering from site to site in the blowing wind and pouring rain. It was great! We had conquered Disney in a hurricane! *(what had once been labeled a hurricane, anyway!)*

Another time, after we were full timers, we were in Salt Springs, Florida, when the same kind of weather system came up out of the Gulf of Mexico. We just stayed at the camper for three days and nights until all the bad weather passed. On the first sunny day we headed south to Kissimmee.

The joy of full timing is that when the weather is miserable outside, we just pay the RV Park for another night and wait for better weather. Now, I'm not saying that we never sight see in bad weather, (sometimes my urge to see new things overcomes my patience to wait for the bad weather to pass) I'm saying that we just don't have to. We are blessed with an abundance of time. It's great to wake up in the morning hearing the rain on the roof and be able to just turn over and go back to sleep! (This would have been great when I had a full time job too!)

Now having been on both sides of the short and long vacation, the only advice I can offer is this: Go on any vacation you can take, be it a short, long, medium, or a weekend, just go. I believe your out look on your job will be better when you get back. Who knows, you might even decide to get a new job when you get back.

Some friends or ours went to Tennessee on vacation and fell in love with the place. All they could talk about was Tennessee when they got back. He and his wife would make the thirteen hour drive back and forth as often as they could. They would even drive up to Tennessee on a Friday and drive back to Louisiana on Sunday! Finally they packed up all their belongings and just moved to Tennessee. They are still in Knoxville to this day and doing far better than they were doing in south Louisiana.

Maybe you will find your new home while out on vacation and maybe not, but in any event a vacation will at the least give you hours of conversation material about where you went and what you saw and what you did.

If you are caught between the 'I should go on vacation and the fifty reasons why you should stay home' I vote **'FOR'** vacation.

And another thing, if you wait for 'extra' money to go on vacation you may have a long wait. I have never found that 'extra' money. We always planed and saved and scrapped up the money to go. That's why we got into camping to start with. Campgrounds are cheaper than motels and hotels and most campers come equipped with a stove, refrigerator, etc. to help curb the cost of those restaurant bills.

What am I trying to tell you? Go out and have a good time! See things you've never seen before, do things you have never done before. Enjoy your life, don't just endure it. Don't be one of the many people that tell me they 'should have' done this or that and now it's too late!

My Mother and Dad had high hopes of retiring and doing a lot of traveling. They spent a lot of time camping in their High Low travel trailer. My Mother was already retired and my Dad had just a few years to go, when he had a severe heart attack and died. If only he could have retired a few years earlier and realized his dreams.

Sometimes we have to **MAKE** our dreams come true. None of us know what is going to happen to us, or our loved ones. None of us can predict what tomorrow will bring. Don't put off what you really want to do. If it's within your reach, grab it!

Now that I've done my part to encourage you to travel, or to do what ever you have dreamed of doing, I'll go on with more of our adventures!

Some friends I met along the way.

Chapter 16: Professional Tourists

We towed our trailer from Five Star Resort in Pass Christian, Mississippi to North of Knoxville, Tennessee, to a place called Mountain Lake Resort. It only took us five days to get there, stopping when we wanted to and enjoying our drive through the beautiful countryside.

We arrived just in time for the 'Homecoming' at the Appalachian Mountain Museum. Homecoming is four days of music and food and more music and more food! We saw all kinds of crafts and many demonstrations of how things were done in the 'old days,' such as splitting rails for fences, making rope, grinding cane to make syrup, and many other things that I won't take time to write about. The pinto beans, cooked over an open, wood fire in a black iron pot, along with the corn bread and onions were marvelous! We had a wonderful time and we decided that we would come to 'Homecoming' again in the future.

We went down to the little community of Townsend, Tennessee and spent a month there. Locals call this the quiet side of the Smoky Mountains. We hiked the trails in the Smoky Mountain National Park, had a lot of picnics and saw some of the most beautiful scenery in the United States. We met a lot of wonderful people and we sure ate a lot of good, country cookin'!

When we arrived in Tennessee the trees were all full of bright green leaves. In just a week they turned into the most magnificent red, orange and yellow colors we have ever seen. Then in another week, it rained and literally all of the leaves fell off the trees. Then the next week it started to snow and about five or six inches accumulated on the ground. We drove across the pass on highway 321 from Townsend through Wear Valley, into Pigeon Forge and then turned onto highway 411 through Gatlinburg and up to Newfound Gap on the Tennessee and North Carolina border. It was the most beautiful winter wonderland. We got out and walked in the snow and took photos until our fingers were numb with the cold and our noses had turned blue! Being from South Louisiana, snow was a very strange thing to us. We had only experienced snow maybe twice in our lives!

In another week, the snow was gone, the sun was out and the weather was beautiful and we headed south to Florida and spent the winter with Mickey. *(You know....Mickey Mouse)*

We did all the theme parks in central Florida, Disney World, Sea World, Cypress Gardens, Busch Gardens, Silver Springs and Universal Studios. We spent the entire winter standing in line! We took our time and saw everything we could see.

In the late 1980's the oil field business fell apart in Louisiana. The economy of the southern part of the state where we lived depended almost entirely on the oil business.

I remember what the Governor said on the evening news. He told us that the state needed to diversify its businesses and try not to depend entirely upon the oil market. One of his suggestions was that we try to further develop the tourist industry. Now my wife and I were doing what the Governor wanted. *We were in the tourist business....we had become professional* tourists!

Our youngest son, Randy, Jr. came to visit us in Florida. He spent a week with us and we did all the *amateur* tourist stuff. You know, we stayed in the lines all day at Disney, instead of just part of the day. His vacation had come to an end and he had to go back to Louisiana to return to work. We drove him to the airport in Orlando and put him on the plane and returned to our camper. My wife began sobbing and sobbing! She was homesick; no she was in grief for our son!

No matter what I did or said didn't seem to help her. She was depressed. I even told her that Randy, Jr. had not died; he had just gone back to Louisiana. Her depression went on for several days and finally I decided to go back to Louisiana, not knowing what else to do. Once the decision was made to go "home," the depression seemed to lift and she was in a lot better spirits. It seemed as though we had discovered what the drawback to being full timers was for us.....we missed the kids!

Although both of our sons were already gone from home when we packed up and left in our RV trailer, there was just something about being across the country and out of touch with them. We were no longer at one permanent location where we could easily be found. Since we didn't have a telephone and no set address, our family members came to think of us as being 'out there' somewhere...and no one knew 'exactly where'. I have to admit that sometimes we did feel like we were out in the middle of no where and not in contact with any one.....and sometimes we were.

We did have an answering service and I called each day to see if any body was looking for us. We hardly ever had a message, but the thought was in our minds that maybe someone had called just a few minutes after we had checked our messages. In short, sometimes we felt really separated from everyone we loved.

It took us about three weeks to drive the eight hundred odd miles back to our old home town. We were reunited with our son and the rest of our family members and friends. We had been on the road for about six months.

I was in the post office and ran across a friend of mine. He came up to me and started telling me how he knew we couldn't stay gone for long. He told me how he had predicted that we wouldn't last long, being out on the road. He just knew it would get old and we would come *crawling* back 'home.' He sure was disappointed when I told him we were just in town for a visit and would soon be gone again. I believe that I ruined his whole day when I told him that. (He is one of those people I was telling you about that won't go any place or do anything.)

We had a nice visit with our family and friends and then we headed out again. We felt better after visiting and we were in high spirits.

We found out that some people evidently don't even realize that you have been gone. What I mean is that when you get back from an extended trip (or sometimes even a short vacation) it seems that some people are not interested in anything you have done, or any place you have been, or in anything you have seen. They know that you have been traveling for an extensive period of time, but they don't ask any questions about anything, or show the least amount of curiosity. They will never bring up the subject of traveling, except to tell you of some horrible experience you missed, because you were gone. They just want to tell you how bad they have been treated at work, why they don't have any money and how sick they have been. They want to make sure you know that nothing has changed.....and how nothing will change! It's as though you have only been gone for fifteen minutes!

A few minutes with one of these people and believe me, you are ready to leave town again and happy to go!

We hitched up and headed north to Arkansas. When we headed out, back on the road, we made a discovery. *(A discovery that seems to hold true for us, if not for everyone else.)* When **we** left there was no sense of being depressed. Sure, we still missed people, but it wasn't the same as when they came to visit us and then **they** left. We still feel this way today and sometimes when we know that family members are coming to visit us in some far away place, we try to time it so that when they leave and go back home, we leave and go some place else too.

So now you know the truth...when you take off, as we did, and start traveling all over the country, you may just miss your family and friends. Wouldn't it be great if you could launch out on your travels and bring those dearest to you along for the trip!

We arrived in Hot Springs, Arkansas and set up our RV at the River View Paradise Camping Resort. We went down town and toured the National park which encompasses Bath House Row. On Bath House Row we toured a restored bath house and walked up and down the streets looking in all the gift shops and restaurants. The next day we went back and actually took one of the baths at the Buck Staff Bath House. It was a good experience, but as a forty four year old man, I didn't like letting another man give me a bath! That was just not my cup of tea. I did enjoy the steam room and the needle shower.

Later we rode the "Duck". A "Duck" is a World War II amphibious vehicle that runs on land or on water. They drove us around town on the paved streets and then they drove off into the lake for a water side tour of the lake front.

After loading all of our plastic gallon jugs with that wonderful water from the hot springs, we headed north and went up to Branson, Missouri.

We stayed in Branson for two weeks. After seeing some of the shows and a day at the Silver Dollar City amusement park, we headed over to Mountain View, Arkansas to attend the dulcimer conference at the Ozark Mountain Folk Center. I play at playing the dulcimer, but I soon found out that what I did know about playing the dulcimer was absolutely NOTHING! We did have a great time and heard some superb music.

Another attraction you don't want to miss while you are in Mountain View is that on the weekends a lot of local musicians show up around the Court House, located in the center of town, and play music. There are usually several groups playing around the square and you can hear good music at absolutely no charge.

A lot of local musicians and singers also perform at the Jimmy Driftwood Theater. There is no charge for this show either, but they will pass the hat. You can't find a better bargain any where.

We left Mountain View and drove up to Eureka Springs, Arkansas. We saw a presentation of the Ozark Hoe Down and went out and saw the Great Passion Play. The Passion Play is something that you do not want to miss if you are in this area. This was the second time my wife and I saw the play.

I went to Eureka Springs with my wife and youngest son and met my Mom and Dad there. We got tickets to the Passion Play and took the bus from the KOA campground to the out door theater where they present the play.

The play was just about over and they were portraying Jesus being hung on the cross when a thunder storm came up. The lightning was flashing and the wind started blowing really hard. The tree branches were bending over almost to the ground. I really thought we were going to get very, very wet. The play ended and there was no rain yet. We all hurriedly headed back to the bus. The bus driver headed back to the campground and all was well. Everyone on the bus was excited about the Passion Play. It was great! Then my Mom made a comment on how realistic the thunder and lightning were at the end of the play! She thought that it was all part of the show!

We left Eureka Springs and headed north west through Oklahoma and into Kansas where we toured Dodge City and saw where the Dalton Gang had 'bought the farm' in Coffeyville. We pulled our travel trailer up to Rapid City, South Dakota.

We saw Mount Rushmore, went to Custer State Park where we literally drove through the buffalo heard and drove up to Deadwood where we saw four or five of the actual chairs in which Wild Bill Hickock was sitting when he was shot! We ate buffalo burgers and saw the giant statue of Crazy Horse, stopped at Wall Drug and drove through the Badlands National Park!

We drove up to Devils Tower in Wyoming and spent a day walking around looking up at all the people that were climbing up to the top. I still get out of breath just thinking about that. (Hanging on a rope a thousand feet off the ground is one of my dreams…a night mare!) We saw where Fort Phil Kearney had been and stopped at Buffalo Bill's hangout in Sheridan, Wyoming.

We drove up into Montana and toured the Custer Battlefield and drove across the state to Gardiner where we camped for a week and drove around in Yellowstone National Park every day.

We were on a roll and we were living our dream. Taking our time and at the same time seeing the sights almost every day. We were calling ourselves 'professional tourists' and we were certainly trying to live up to our new titles!

After spending four or five days in Yellowstone National Park and after seeing 'Old Faithful,' the great buffalo herd and hundreds of elk, we decided to drive up the Bear Tooth Highway. We were driving along side the frozen lake and in some places the snow looked like it was about twenty feet deep on the side of the road. I had just a little over 'zero' experience in driving on frozen roads and after we saw a snow plow on the side of the road, I began wondering if I should turn around and go back. I didn't have any tire chains and if I had had some, I wouldn't have known what to do with them. I spotted a gift shop and gas station and I pulled over. I went into the gift shop and I explained to the man behind the counter that I was from Louisiana and that I didn't have any experience driving in winter conditions. I asked him if he thought we should continue on or if we should turn around and go back.

"You said you're from Louisiana?" he asked. I answered that I was. He asked, "Have you ever crossed over the Huey P. Long Bridge in New Orleans?" I told him yes, that I had driven across that bridge many times. He said, "There ain't nothin' up here that scary!" *(If you have ever driven across that bridge, you probably know what he meant.)*

We went on and drove the highway. It's one of the only highways were the road goes over the peak of the mountain and not below it. It is a wonderfully gorgeous drive. Bear Tooth Pass is almost 11,000 feet above sea level.

We left Gardiner and crossed the state of Idaho. We stopped over at the Lewis and Clark Resort in Kamiah. We saw the "Heart of the Monster" on the Nez Perce reservation.

We cut down through Washington State and pulled our trailer along the Columbia River. One day the wind was blowing extremely hard and we were headed right into it. I had the Suburban floor boarded and we were only doing about forty five miles per hour. The gas mileage went down the drain that day!

We pulled into Turner, Oregon, which is right out of Salem and spent a week visiting our oldest son who was living in Dallas, Oregon at the time. We visited Silver Falls and spent a day fishing from a float boat drifting down the Santiam River. I never caught any fish, but the trip was well worth the effort. The scenery was magnificent and I thoroughly enjoyed floating down the river in that beautiful, crystal clear, water.

Everything was going well and I decided to have the transmission serviced on our Chevrolet Suburban. I had about 90,000 miles on the vehicle. The transmission man pulled the pan on the transmission and then called me over to see all the shinny pieces of metal that spelled out **'EXPENSIVE TRANSMISSION REPAIR'**! They did the job in two days and after forking over $1,270.00 we were on our way again.

My wife and I had decided to go to Alaska. I can remember my Dad talking with one of his friends about the Alaska Highway when I was a kid and I had always longed to go up and take a look at it.

At first I thought that we would leave our travel trailer at my son's house in Oregon. I had gone to Bass Pro Shop in Springfield, Missouri and purchased a large tent that fastened to the back end of the Chevy Suburban. I bought an air mattress that fit snugly in the back end of our vehicle and with the tent attached you could crawl out the back end of the truck and you would be inside the tent. I also purchased a Coleman propane stove, a Coleman propane lantern, and a port-a-potty.

My wife never did like the idea of camping in the back end of our Suburban and no matter what size tent I had, it didn't satisfy her. She wanted to take the bathroom with her and the bathroom was built inside the rear end of our Coachmen RV travel trailer.

She was afraid of snakes and although I told her that there are no snakes in Alaska, she still could not be convinced that camping in the tent would be a lot of fun.

I decided to 'pitch' the tent one day to show her how much room we would have and how comfy' we would be. After about an hour I finally had the thing put together. It sure was a lot of **'fun'** assembling that tent and attaching it to the back end of the Suburban! When we arrived in Oregon, I gave the tent and the port-a-potty to my son and we hooked the trailer to the Suburban and we were off, this time headed north.

Chapter 17: North to Alaska

We headed north on I-5 and drove through Washington state and crossed the border into Canada at Sumas. We continued on and stopped to see the attraction at Hell's Gate, where we rode the cable car down to the river and looked in all the shops. We drove into Cache Creek, British Columbia and stopped for the night. We had driven through some of the most beautiful country we had ever been in. We were having a wonderful time, even if the price of gasoline was $2.23 a gallon (Canadian money)

The next day we drove up to Ten Mile Lake. We stopped on the way at the 108 Mile House. There were some turn of the century serial murderers that ran a hotel there and had killed some of the miners that were returning from the gold fields in the Yukon. They told us a very interesting story of what had happened there and how the murderers had eventually been caught red handed. *(I still don't know how these people could have been serial murderers without having a TV set to show them how to do it!)*

We went on to Lake Tudyah and stopped for the night at the Provincial Park. The Park is located on a big lake and is in a beautiful setting. I got out my rod and reel and put a little spinner bait on to see if I could catch any fish. I walked down to the edge of the lake and saw a man standing there fishing. I started up a conversation with him. He asked me what kind of bait I was going to fish with and I showed him the little spinner bait. He told me that I had the wrong kind of bait, it was the wrong color and that I had to have some certain bait that he named. I had never heard of that kind of bait before and assumed that it was something sold in Canada. I started to fish and caught fish after fish after fish! I kept an eye on the other guy and observed that he had not caught a thing. After a while, he reeled in his line and was gone. This was the kind of place I had read about and expected British Columbia to be. I don't even know what kind of fish I was catching, only that I caught a lot of them and put them right back into the lake where they came from.

My wife had taken a lawn chair, walked down to the lake and was sitting there reading her Bible. A large flock of Canadian Geese began to circle us. They flew around and around us. I was enjoying this greatly, because I had never been this close to wild geese before. All of a sudden they landed **ALL AROUND MY WIFE!** I couldn't believe it! These geese evidently had no fear of humans. They walked all around my wife coming within a foot of her, sitting there in her lawn chair. There are three sizes of Canadian geese, I found out later, and these were the largest variety.

They were in no hurry to leave and walked all around my wife and came to the edge of the water where I was fishing. (I had on rubber boots and was a little ways out in the lake.) In south Louisiana where we were from you had to look quickly to see wild life, before the wild life ran off to get away from you. I truly had a sense of being in the wilderness from this experience.

The next day we headed off to Dawson Creek. On the way our Suburban engine started missing. There was no place to stop so we just continued on. The farther we went the more the engine sputtered and popped. We arrived in Chetwynd and I pulled up at a gas station. The nice people in the station got on the telephone and started calling around trying to find a mechanic. It was Saturday afternoon and they had a little trouble getting anyone to respond. Finally, I was told that someone was on the way to help me.

A few minutes later a man arrived in a pick up truck and after a little conversation he told me to follow him and I did. We drove to his mechanic shop and in just a few minutes he was under the hood. After he replaced two burned spark plug wires and I gave the mechanic $70.00 we were off again. We pulled into Dawson Creek at Tubby's Camp Ground.

We didn't know it at the time, but Tubby's is the place where a lot of the Alaska Caravans depart from. Almost everyone in the campground was signed up with a caravan. We felt a little guilty, because we were going to drive the Alaska Highway on our own.

We did our laundry *(even professional tourists get their clothes dirty)* and did some grocery shopping. Later in the afternoon, we were sitting outside of our trailer in our lawn chairs. People walked by, told us "Hello" and just about every one of them asked us if we were signed up with a caravan. Some of our new neighbors just couldn't understand why we wanted to go up the highway on our own. I told them that the caravan was on a schedule and that I wanted to take my time and go at my own pace. Then one guy asked me, "What happens if you break down in the middle of no where? What will you do then?"

I told him that in the event that I would break down, I'd just pull over to the side of the road and get out and open the hood and see if I could correct the problem. If I couldn't, I'd wait for someone to come along that would give me a hand. I knew that all the caravans have what they call a 'tail gunner' following along behind them and most of the time the tail gunners (rear scouts) had some mechanical ability. I figured that someone would stop and give us a hand, or get us in touch with someone who would. The man who was questioning me agreed with me that someone would probably stop and help.

Although we were sitting there in Dawson Creek, British Columbia at the zero milepost of the Alaska Highway and we were ready to head north, there was still a little apprehension on our part. While sitting around the campground, we heard some of the tales of terror associated with traveling the highway. We heard of transmissions falling out on the road, of refrigerators being torn out of walls and tires blowing out, wheels falling off and broken windshields. I have to admit that a few times I wondered just what in the world we were getting into. Could the highway really be that bad? And if it was, why were so many people so excited about driving it? I knew the answer...it was the last great driving adventure on this continent! As professional tourists we **HAD** to go!

We were as prepared as we knew how to get. We had a spare tire for the trailer and one for the Suburban; we had filled up the fresh water tank and emptied the black and gray water tanks. I had my tool box and I even had a package of tire plugs just in case we had some of those flat tires every one talked about. We were well stocked up on groceries and had exchanged our American money for Canadian money. We had bought our copy of the Milepost Magazine (The Milepost is a magazine...a really thick magazine...published each year and gives you a mile by mile description of the Alaska Highway and all the roads in Alaska and in Northern British Columbia, Yukon and Northwest Territories. If you plan to travel in this part of the world, then the Milepost is a MUST) and we had our road map. I mean, even for the guy who has trouble with road maps, this was going to be simple. There was only one road!

Ignoring the pleas of the folks we met to join up with one of the caravans, we were off.

We left Tubby's and Dawson Creek behind and drove through Fort St. John and decided to stop at the Prophet River Provincial Park for the night. We set up and got our lawn chairs out and made us a nice campfire. The Provincial Parks provide free fire wood, but they have no hook ups in their campgrounds.

We were 'boon-docking' or camping with no electric or water hook ups. This was **'real'** adventure for us. My youngest son used to tease us about how we were 'roughing it' with the microwave, the color TV and VCR. We wished he could see us now with no electricity!

My wife decided that she wanted to cook some pinto beans. We had been sitting outside, so I got out our brand new Coleman propane stove, put it on a picnic table and my wife prepared the beans to be cooked in our pressure cooker. We had the pressure regulator on the cooker jingling in no time. My wife was in and out of the camper doing what ever wives do when you are just relaxing around the campfire and the stove is cooking up something good. I put myself in charge of keeping the stove adjusted so the pressure regulator on the pressure cooker was jingling just right. My wife kept telling me to leave the thing alone, but I knew better. After all this was the first time I had had a chance to play with my new stove. My wife had been cooking in that pressure cooker for years and now it was my turn to play with it.

Well, I don't know exactly what happened, but all of a sudden the pressure relief valve blew out of the pressure cooker! A geyser of white steam and water ten feet high was screaming out of the lid on that pot! I jumped over to the stove and hurriedly screwed the knob down on the stove to extinguish the flame. Once that was done, all I could do was wait for the geyser to subside, which it did in a short time.

Needless to say, my wife was 'overjoyed' with the way I had handled the cooking chores that day! After the pot had cooled down, I took the top off and found out that only the water had escaped from the pot…the beans were still in there! A little more cooking and they were quite delicious! I cleaned up the mess and tranquility once more encompassed our campsite.

A couple of hours later we were sitting outside, enjoying the campfire when a man came walking up. We started chatting and then he said, "I see your propane bottle gave you some trouble a while ago." I didn't know what he was talking about and I told him that I didn't have any trouble like that. He said, "Well, I saw a white cloud coming off your gas bottle by the picnic table. I was glad that nothing caught on fire." I still didn't know what he was talking about until I thought about the pressure cooker. I told him that it wasn't a propane leak; it was our pinto beans blowing out of our pressure cooker. He looked a little disgusted and told me, "Now I sat there in my motor home and got sick from smelling that propane gas and now I find out that it wasn't propane gas at all, just pinto beans!"

I guess if your mind tells you one thing and you don't know any better, the rest of your body will react accordingly.

The next morning we were back on the road. We passed raging rivers, calm lakes and trickling streams. Sometimes the road was paved and sometimes the road was gravel. Sometimes the gravel road was better to drive on than the 'paved' road was. We saw a lot of dust when the road was dry and a lot of mud when the road was wet. We were adventurers on a great adventure! We were trying to do the smart thing, so we slowed down when the road got bad and speeded up a little when the road got better.

I stopped on the side of the road and caught two Arctic Grayling fish and the mosquitoes almost carried my wife and I off into the woods. We put the fish back into the water and ran back to the Suburban for cover.

We saw the great Sign Forrest in Watson Lake, Yukon Territory. There are thousands and thousands of every kind of sign you can imagine. Any one who wants to put up a sign can do so and there are signs from all over the world here. There is also on display one of the aircraft that the United States gave to Russia in World War II. Many of these planes "flew" up the highway, where they were turned over to Russian pilots to be flown back to the battle fields in Russia.

We stopped at Mukluk Annie's where you can camp for free and they have a salmon bake every night. For a side trip, we drove sixty-five miles down a gravel road to Atlin, British Columbia. Atlin is on the edge of a big lake and the snow covered mountains seem to go straight up out of the lake. The scenery is breath taking!

We drove up to Whitehorse, the capital of the Yukon Territory. We toured the steamboat, 'Klondike,' and saw the weather vane at the airport that is made out of a DC-3 airplane! We bought more groceries, toured the museums and visited the reindeer farm north of town.

Then we made a decision to leave the Alaska Highway. We turned north from Whitehorse and headed to Dawson City, the site of the 1898 gold rush. It's about 325 miles from Dawson City to Whitehorse, all on a nice paved road.

It took us two days to get to Dawson City. We pulled up into a campground that actually had electric hook ups. Well sort of. If you tried to turn on anything except the TV, the circuit breaker would kick off. I don't know how many times I had to go outside and flip that circuit breaker back on. It was very frustrating to say the least and I won't go into any details on what names I called that circuit breaker.

We did all the Yukon gold rush stuff, visited the Bonanza Creek where gold was discovered, took a walking tour of downtown and saw where all the houses of ill repute used to be, toured the Commissioners Mansion, saw a film at the Palace Grand Theater, took the boat tour to the steam boat graveyard on the Yukon River, drove up to the dome, (a mountain overlooking the river and Dawson City), went to the cabin where Robert Service, (a great poet) used to live, went to see the Gold Dredge #4 and ate salmon chowder at Nancy's Restaurant.

Dawson City is a very interesting place. The paved road ends at the city limits and none of the streets are paved. They still have board sidewalks and a lot of the original buildings are still standing, just as they were during the gold rush. Being a history buff, I greatly enjoyed walking the streets of Dawson City.

We went to see Jack London's cabin. My wife stepped off the sidewalk into a hole in the ground and twisted her ankle badly. The ankle was swollen and hurt her so much that our walking tours were abruptly ended. *(No, we didn't sue them!)* We didn't get a chance to go to the casino at Diamond Tooth Gerties, but we did drive about seventy-five miles up the Dempster Highway toward the Northwest Territories. We got our first look at the tundra and the beautiful scenery along the road.

We decided to take the Top of the World Highway back to the Alaska Highway, instead of going all the way back to Whitehorse. The Top of the World Highway is just what it sounds like. The highway meanders along the peaks of the mountains. You drive on top of the world! The road is one hundred and sixty five miles of dirt and gravel. It's not very good in some places. Beautiful does not adequately describe the scenery. It is breath taking.

We drove on a nice, dry, day and the traffic was not very heavy, but I'll bet it would not have been as pleasurable if it had been raining and we had been driving along in the mud! Where the road was not good, we just slowed down and took our time. *(This is the secret to keeping everything in one piece.)* We drove along, stopping to take photographs and even had a roadside picnic.

We crossed the border at Boundary, Alaska. After answering the usual questions, we were back in the USA.

(We have driven the Top of the World highway in the rain and mud and believe me.....dry is better. Now a lot of this road has been paved and it is a lot easier driving than it was the first time we traveled it in 1992. The road is paved from Dawson City to the Alaska Border and back from the Alaska Highway for some miles north toward Chicken. There is still enough of the dirt and gravel road to satisfy our adventurous spirit!)

Mud gets everywhere and into everything!

Chapter 18: The Great Land

We had finally made it to Alaska! We were still on a bad, gravel and dirt road headed to Tok, *(pronounced like Coke)* to get back on the Alaska Highway.

We came into Chicken, Alaska and stopped at the Gold Panner. The Gold Panner is a gas station and store and the owner let us 'boon dock' free behind the store building. *(There is a charge for camping at the Gold Panner now)* Chicken Creek runs through the property and gold panning is allowed.

I set up the rig and borrowed a gold pan from the front porch of the store and walked down to the creek. There were a few other people "washing gravel" along the side of the creek. I knew as much about gold panning as I did about flying jet fighters, so I just kind of stood there and watched the others. I knew that gold was heavier than the rocks and dirt it was buried in and by washing the dirt and rocks off with water, the gold was supposed to settle to the bottom of the pan. But I didn't know what the gold was supposed to look like. I had seen a guy in the movies once that had spent days in a mine doing back breaking work, only to find out that he was mining fools gold. I didn't want to start panning fools gold and look like a fool, so I watched the other people that were panning in the creek some more. This was another new thing to me. There was not a lot of gold prospecting being done in south Louisiana when I lived there.

I noticed right off that some of the folks on the creek knew about as much as I did about panning. There was one couple however, a young man and his wife, that really seemed to know what was going on. They seemed to waste no effort and they knew how to work the water over the material in their pans quickly and efficiently. Being a very shy person, it took me about ten seconds to walk right up and ask them to show me how to pan for gold. His name was Wayne Singer and I remember that he worked for the singer Eric Clapton, but his hobby was gold prospecting. He took his time and showed me how to put the material (dirt and rocks) in the pan and wash it off with the water that was running in the creek. And as I washed and washed, *(I was really slow at doing this)* he kept his eye on me and gave me a little instruction from time to time. Then he leaned over and pointed out the **GOLD IN MY PAN!!!!!** It was beautiful, it was gorgeous, and it was about the size of a *very small* grain of sand! But it was gold. I learned a lesson that day. Once you see gold in the bottom of your pan, you will never mistake fools gold for the real thing.

I don't remember Wayne's wife's name, but she knew some tricks about panning too and wasn't hesitant about sharing her knowledge. I went on to find several "nuggets" there at Chicken Creek. It was one of the high points of my first Alaskan adventure. I have spent time in Arizona, Yukon Territory, and Nova Scotia and in other parts of Alaska panning for gold since this first lesson. It is hard, back breaking work and those gold rushers of by gone days earned every cent they took out of those creeks and streams. I still enjoy doing a little prospecting. Some folks really get taken up in the hunt for gold and 'gold fever' is still a contagious disease today!

My wife on the other hand couldn't find the recreational value of digging a hole in the ground with a shovel.

We left Chicken and headed down to the Alaska Highway. There is a place in the road that is referred to in the Milepost Magazine as 'stabilized sand dunes.' We were traveling down the road at about thirty-five miles an hour when the road went around a curve and then suddenly down a steep hill. The trailer tried to pass up the Suburban! I don't mind telling you that my heart skipped several beats! I reached down and activated the trailer brake and the trailer swung back behind the Suburban where it was supposed to be. I was very relieved to get back to the Alaska Highway and onto a paved road.

We pulled into the Tok visitors' center and saw some tourist films and bought an annual Alaska Parks camping pass. With this pass you can camp for the rest of the summer in all of the State Parks for no additional charge. *(Alaska has discontinued the annual pass program…darn it!)* You have to 'boon dock' in the parks since there are no hook ups, but usually potable water is available and lots of beautiful scenery to make up for the lack of electricity. We have used an annual camping pass every summer we have spent in Alaska and find it to be a great value.

We stopped in Delta Junction which is the official end of the Alaska Highway. The road between Delta Junction and Fairbanks was already in existence when work was started to extend the road into British Columbia in 1942, so the road between Delta Junction and Dawson Creek, British Columbia is the road built during World War II and is what we call the Alaska Highway or the Al-Can Highway. *(Alaska-Canada Highway)*

We went to the visitors' center and saw the displays. There is a "Pig" on display which was very interesting. A Pig is the devise that is sent through the Alaska Pipeline to clean it out. It doesn't look like a real pig and I don't know how it got its name.

We got our first look at the Alaska Pipeline where it crosses the Tanana River. It is an engineering marvel. But, what else can I say...it's a pipe. A very long pipe indeed, but it's still a pipe. In southern Louisiana these pipe lines are every where and I really don't pay them a lot of attention, but we were glad to get a look at this one since it is so famous.

We headed out toward Fairbanks. We drove through the most marvelous country side. We saw beautiful mountains and lakes and streams. We saw six moose on the side of the road in one morning! Speaking of wildlife, we learned some things by traveling up 'the highway.'

First of all, if you come upon a herd of Caribou and they are on both sides of the highway, proceed very, very slowly. You will notice that all of the Caribou on the right side of the road will cross over to the left side of the road and all of the Caribou on the left side of the road will cross over to the right side of the road, all right in front of your vehicle. After all of them have crossed the road, it is usually pretty safe to **slowly** proceed on your way. I say slowly because some of them might cross back over to the side of the road where they came from to begin with. You never know what a Caribou will do!

We have also come upon Stone Sheep that appear to be eating the highway. They are in reality not eating the highway, but are licking up the salt (and no telling what else) that was put on the roadway in the winter, because of the ice and snow. Some of these sheep will not get out of your way! Hunters spend thousands of dollars and go miles out into the wilderness to hunt these sheep, but here they are, blocking the road.....at no additional charge.

Arctic squirrels will wait until you are dead even with them and then run right across the road in front of you. You can usually see some of the remains of the slow ones still on the road. If you keep an eye up the road as you drive, you can usually spot them up ahead standing on their two hind legs at attention waiting to dash out when you get there. I don't know what to tell you to do about it, other than to just be aware of it.

Another animal that can be viewed in several places along the route is Dahl Sheep. South of Anchorage on the Seward Highway these sheep come down from their mountain homes right to the edge of the road and cause traffic jams in the summer. They don't seem to have any fear of humans, but they also live in a protected area where no hunting is allowed.

After I had been in Alaska for awhile, I discovered that the tourists are afraid of the Grizzly Bears and the Alaskans are afraid of the Moose. It seems that the bears 'usually' mind their own business around people, unless you happen upon a bear that is feeding. A feeding bear will fight you to protect its food. *(For a sample of what to expect, go to the Royal Fork Buffet in Anchorage and get in front of some one in the food line!)*

A moose on the other hand will go out of its way to start some trouble with you. I don't know what makes them mad at people, but they sure do go on a rampage sometimes. People have even been killed right in Anchorage by these animals. And if you happen to have a dog with you, a moose will go far out of his way to try to stomp your dog. They are beautiful animals, but view them with caution. They will stand in the road and block your passage. Leave them alone! They **WILL** attack your vehicle!

Now don't get me wrong. I'm not a moose hater. To the contrary I love moose and I love to hunt them. I shoot them with my camera! But I'm just telling you this because a lot of people go to Alaska and think that they are in a petting zoo. Enjoy the wild life, but remember that the wild life is **WILD!** After a moose chased me around the parking lot at Russian Jack Springs Park in Anchorage, I am very cautious and attentive when I'm in moose country.

We drove on up the road and stopped at the Knotty Shop, a really neat gift shop just south of North Pole. If you are gift hunting this might be a good place for you to stop.

We stopped at Santa's house in North Pole. Sure enough Santa was there to welcome us and although this was the end of June, it was still Christmas at North Pole. This is about the biggest Christmas store I have ever seen. You can stop and sign up for Santa to send a personal letter to the kids in your family when the 'real' Christmas season comes and the letter will be postmarked North Pole, Alaska.

We arrived in Fairbanks and set the rig up at the Chena River State Park. The park is right in Fairbanks and not far from Alaska Land where you can learn about the history of Fairbanks and see a lot of arts and crafts.

We took a side trip to the Gold Dredge #8 and enjoyed the tour. They explained how the gold dredge worked and all the things that had to be done to mine the gold with this equipment. The dredges were so large that they were just abandoned when the gold played out and there are several of the dredges that can be seen throughout Alaska and in the Yukon.

Gold panning is also allowed at Gold Dredge #8 and I did find another couple of "nuggets." The employees there are willing and able to show you how to work the pan and I picked up a few helpful hints from them to add to what I learned while panning on Chicken Creek.

We left the travel trailer at Chena River Park and took the Suburban up the "Haul Road." That's the name the locals have given to the Dalton Highway. The Dalton Highway runs all the way to the Arctic Ocean on Prudhoe Bay. We didn't go all the way up to the ocean. At this time the road was restricted and travel was not allowed all the way up. I understand that the road is open to the general public now and travelers can drive all the way past Coldfoot to Prudhoe Bay.

We drove up and crossed the Yukon River and drove out into the tundra and on to the Arctic Circle. There is a picnic area at the circle and a fancy sign so you will know where you are. My wife and I decided to have a picnic. I could see mosquitoes swarming outside the Suburban, so I got out the mosquito repellent and we both rubbed some on. We got out of the car and started getting our picnic supplies out and hauling them to the near by table. The mosquitoes attacked us with a vengeance! We must have been the first meat they had seen in a while. The repellent was **NOT** working at all! I believe that these giant mosquitoes were being attracted by it! There was no way we could stay out there with all those blood sucking pests. We had to escape. Then my wife decided that she had to go.....you know, to the restroom. Well, there were some outdoor toilets (outhouses) there, but some kind, considerate, gentle soul had made a mess so bad on the floor that you couldn't get in without hip boots, so I told her to go behind the bushes. There probably wasn't another person around for fifty miles any way. She went behind that bush and proceeded to be attacked by a hundred million thirsty bugs! *(I'll bet they thought the moon had come out when they saw that white shinning behind, out in the open air!)*

We ran to the Suburban and got in. We spent the next ten minutes swatting the mosquitoes that had followed us into the vehicle. We swatted the stragglers for another two hours. We went north for a few miles and then turned around and headed back to Fairbanks. We had set out to cross the Arctic Circle and that being accomplished we drove south, scratching our insect bites.

We stopped at the restaurant and gift shop at the Yukon River Bridge and ate chili and got our certificates to show that we had crossed the Arctic Circle. Mosquitoes aside, we had another lovely, adventurous day.

We had driven about four hundred miles of gravel road and didn't get back to our rig until about midnight. The sun was still up! This time of the year (summer) the sun shines almost twenty-four hours a day, so you really don't have to spend a lot of time planning where you will be come sundown. I have spoken to people who say they don't know if they would like the sun to be up all day and all night. The people who say this usually have never experienced these never ending days. I love them! You can go fishing at 3:00 AM! You can take a ride looking for wildlife after the nightly news and it's still day light.

You can sit outside and talk to your neighbor in the campground at midnight.

We were in a provincial park at Liard Hot Springs in British Columbia. It was almost one AM and we were going to bed. I was pulling down the shade and I looked out the window and the guy next door was just firing up his Bar-B-Q pit! His kids were riding their bikes and playing and having a wonderful time. The sun was out and they evidently had no idea of the time. If you want to get the most out of your 'sunny' vacation then this is the place for you!

We toured the museum at the University of Alaska at Fairbanks and from their observation platform we saw Mt. McKinley for the first time. When the weather is clear and the mountain is 'out' you can see it from Fairbanks and Anchorage. The mountain is 20,320 feet high. It is a real treat to be able to see the mountain. I'm told that only about twenty-five percent of the tourists that come to Alaska see Mt. McKinley. Even on clear days the mountain sometimes makes its own weather and may be shrouded in clouds. The local people refer to the mountain as Denali, the name the native people gave it.

We drove into Denali Park and signed up for the bus tour. Private vehicles are only allowed to drive a portion of the road into the park and if you want to see more you have to ride the bus to do it. The buses are just like school buses that are pressed into park service in the summer. They are very uncomfortable, and the way that the windows are made you would think that the designer was attempting to stop you from seeing anything. I have made the trip by bus to the Eielson Visitor center, which is about sixty-five miles into the park, twice. You have to bring your own food and drink with you. There are no eating facilities in the park once you leave the main visitors center.

The first time I went into the park the weather was fairly nice and we saw a lot of moose, caribou and even about a half dozen grizzly bears. We saw fox and coyote and Dahl sheep, but the most memorable part of the trip was the bus wheels hanging off the edge of the road in Polychrome Pass! The road is gravel and one lane and some of the road passes through places where there is a rock wall going straight up on one side and a drop off of hundreds of feet, *maybe thousands of feet,* on the other side. And there we were on this one lane road with two school buses passing each other! The scenery was GREAT and I guess that's why we went back a second time on another of our Alaska journeys.

The second time around I believe that the bus seats had gotten harder! It was drizzling rain and rocks were rolling down the side of the mountains onto the roadway. There was a woman driver and tour guide and she thought she was supposed to look back at all the people and talk while she drove down that narrow, winding road on the side of that cliff! Because of the rain everyone had put the windows up and they soon became so fogged up that you couldn't see anything except the driver looking back at us as she drove forward down the road of terror!

There was a guy sitting in front of me and I could see that he was visibly shaken by all this and I'm sure that if he would have looked back at me he would have seen that I was visibly shaken also. *(There is just something about waiting to plunge downward a thousand feet off the side of a cliff in an uncomfortable school bus, headed down a bumpy gravel road that's only about a foot wider than the bus, which is being driven by a complete stranger, who continuously looks back at you, instead of at the road, that tends to unnerve me!)* I told him that I believed that there was more praying going on in that bus than there was in most churches on Sunday. He replied to me that he didn't know about that, but that he had sure been praying!

My wife was sitting in the window seat and we were riding on the curb side of the bus. She told me to look out the window. I could tell by her voice that I didn't want to look out the window. She told me several times to look and I just ignored her. She was persistent and finally I told her that I didn't want to look out. She said, "You can't see the road at all when you look down. The side of the bus is hanging off the cliff!" That was all I needed to hear at this particular time.

We did get back safely with no problems except for the strain on our hearts and my knuckles were white for three hours after I got off the bus from squeezing the seat in the front of me. If you want to see a lot of wildlife and some of the most beautiful, untouched, country on our continent, then I advise you to take the shuttle bus into Denali Park. It will be an unforgettable trip. You will see lots of animals and I'll gladly wait for you at the park entrance...probably in the restaurant at the park hotel. I'll be sitting near the rest rooms.

We drove into Anchorage and stopped at three RV Parks and each time were advised that they were full. Finally, one of the campground employees told me that a lot of campers parked behind the Dimond Mall on Dimond Blvd., on the southern side of the city. He gave me directions and we pulled the trailer there and to our surprise there must have been two hundred RVs in the lot. It was just a big field that was partially covered with gravel.

(Wal-Mart has come to town and now occupies this site, but in the summer you can still find many happy campers parked there. I came to Anchorage in 1994 and we parked at the new, Wal-Mart. I called both of our sons and told them that their mother was in Hog Heaven....she was living at Wal Mart!)

We toured the city and saw the sites and the gift shops. We ate some really good Chinese food. There seems to be one Chinese restaurant in every square block of the town. We went

144

to the museums and shopped for fur coats on Fourth Ave. We didn't buy any, though my wife eyed up a few of them pretty closely.

We left Anchorage and drove about forty miles south to Portage Glacier. This is the most visited tourist site in Alaska and we didn't want to be the first "Professional Tourists" not to show up.

The Boggs-Begich Visitors Center is located here and we got to see ice worms for the first time. Yes they are real! They are little, teeny-tiny worms that live in the glacier ice. *(Kind of makes you not want to eat any of the ice, doesn't it?)* We took a boat and went across the lake, dodging all the icebergs until the glacier came into view. It was impressive. A giant, ice wall as tall as a ten story building! The ice in the glacier is a beautiful blue color and you can see some of the rest of the glacier as it winds its way up the side of the mountain.

We headed to Seward and followed the camping signs down to the beach when we got there. The 'beach' is mostly rocks and gravel and there were a lot of RVs there already. There were no hook ups, but we were becoming good at 'boon-docking' camping. We learned to conserve water and to sleep without the air conditioner running. It's cool there and you don't need air conditioning, but I like the sound the fan makes and it puts me to sleep. We set up the trailer in the campground and got tickets to take the boat into the Kenai Fjords National Park.

The next day we boarded the boat and went into the park. **This is a *GREAT* boat trip!** We saw whales, sea otters, Puffins, eagles, sea lions and ate crab and shrimp on the tour boat! We saw a lot of glaciers and the scenery was fantastic!

After a good nights sleep, we went to the museum. They showed us a very interesting film on the 1964 earthquake. The film showed the devastation caused by several tidal waves that swept ashore as a result of the earthquake. When we were leaving the exhibit I asked the girl behind the sales counter about the film. I asked her where the tidal waves had swept ashore. She said. "Do you know where they park all those campers over on the beach?" I told her that I did and that I had my camper parked there now. "That's where the waves came ashore," she replied. That night when I got in bed, I thought about those waves crashing ashore a long time before I went to sleep!

Icebergs in Portage Lake, Alaska.

Hanging glacier in Alaska.

ARCTIC CIRCLE CROSSING CERTIFICATE

TO ALL TO WHOM THESE LETTERS SHALL COME GREETINGS
BE IT KNOWN THAT _____ ON
THIS ___ DAY OF _____ 19__ HAS VENTURED
THE RIGORS OF THE FROZEN ARCTIC AND CROSSED OVER
THE ARCTIC CIRCLE, 66 DEGREES - 33 MINUTES
NORTH OF THE EQUATOR AND IS HEREBY AWARDED THIS
CERTIFICATE OF ACCOMPLISHMENT.
SIGNED _____

Up close to an Alaskan glacier.

The start of the Alaska Highway

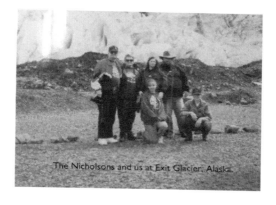

The Nicholsons and us at Exit Glacier, Alaska

Mama Pat melting ice with her butt.

Chapter 19: Fishing

We put Seward behind us and went back up to Soldotna. The Kenai River runs through this town and the river is famous for all the giant King Salmon caught there. The largest caught so far has exceeded ninety pounds.

We pulled into Morgan's Landing State Park and set the rig up. I grabbed my rod and reel and we walked down to the river. There were a few people fishing along the bank of the river. I had already purchased some 'flies' to fish with. At first when I was told that I needed to fish with artificial flies, I was somewhat disappointed, because I didn't have a fly rod. I thought I was going to have to purchase some new equipment, but I found out that Alaska 'fly' fishing consisted of a good bait casting reel, thirty pound test line and a 'fly' that is built on a big hook and a half ounce weight placed above the fly... to give it balance.

On my first outing I took the fly and cast it out into the river as far as I could cast it. I must have made hundreds of casts and finally I caught a nice, shinny Sockeye Salmon. This was to be the only fish I would catch for several days and even though I would fish intently, each day I came home empty handed. I saw other fishermen coming down the trail with their limit of salmon on their stringers. I thought that they were just having better luck than I was having, or that perhaps they were fishing in a better spot. I always thought I would do better the next time, but the next time I still caught nothing.

Then on about the fourth day, I caught another salmon. Now, I really believed that it was just a matter of being in the right place at the right time and so far my timing or my place had been off.

I took my wife walking down the path that follows the river and of course I brought our fishing gear with us. My wife does NOT like to fish. She really likes to clean fish, but she doesn't like to catch them. Don't ask me why.

Back in the late '70's, I took June to fish the marsh ponds and lakes in southern Louisiana. Mr. Herbert Lee, a good friend of mine, was our guide. Mr. Lee was a trapper and knew the marsh like the back of his hand. He knew that June didn't like to fish and he was out to change her mind. He put her up in the front of his boat and advised me that he and I were not going to fish that day. It was June's day to catch the fish.

He would pull up to a point of land, or a sunken log and tell my wife to "throw" over to some certain place he was pointing out. My wife could work a spin casting rig pretty good and she would follow his instructions. She was fishing with top water bait and just about the time that bait would hit the water a three or four pound bass would attack with a vengeance. She went on to catch eight or ten good sized bass and we were only out for a short time.

I put her back in my boat and when we were on our way back to the landing I asked her, "Wasn't that fun? What do you think of fishing now?"

"Well, it was OK, but I just don't like to fish," she said.

I couldn't believe it. Some fishermen would pay thousands of dollars to go on the kind of fishing trip she had just been on and now she was telling me she didn't like to fish! This just didn't make any sense at all to a Cajun boy like me.

So we stopped at a picturesque spot on the bank of the Kenai River and I prepared her line. I knew that she didn't like to fish, but I figured that once she hooked into one of those hard fighting Sockeyes, she would surely change her mind. I put a 'fly' on her rod which was equipped with a push button spin cast reel. I had changed the line to eighteen or twenty pound test. It was about the heaviest test line that the reel would take and still operate properly. I set the drag as tight as I could so that the fish wouldn't pull a lot of line out of the reel. With the heavier line the reel capacity had been some what reduced. I showed her how to work the line in the water, which was the wrong way to work the line, but I thought I was right at the time. In no time at all she had hooked a good fish. The fish was pulling and I was yelling instructions! I could see that the yelling of the instructions was not having a pleasing effect on her at all. She had on a pair of those leather shoes, the kind with the smooth soles. That fish was pulling and pulling and if you have ever hooked into one of these fish, then you know what I mean when I say that they pull hard! The pulling of the fish combined with the river current really tugs on the line. She was standing in some soft, wet mud and suddenly she started slipping into the river. The river was roaring by with a very strong current and the water was very COLD! You should have seen the look on her face in that two seconds that she thought she was going to be pulled overboard! But she stopped sliding and resumed the fight with the fish and then her line broke.

She reeled it in and I put on another fly and weight and she was back in business. After a few more casts, she had another fish hooked! The battle was on again. She pulled and pulled and that salmon pulled and pulled. Then, her line broke again!

She turned around, facing me and looking very disgusted said, "Here!" and handed me the rod. I started to get out another fly, but she halted me. "I'm not going to stand here fishing all day when every time I get a fish he breaks my line. I quit!"

"What do you mean, you quit? The fish are running and you hooked two of them in no time and now you want to quit?" I responded in disbelief. It had taken me four or five days to hook two fish.

"It's no fun fishing anyway. I don't want to fish any more. I want to go back to the camper," was her reply.

I slowly picked up our gear and headed back up the path toward the travel trailer.

As I was slowly walking along the trail trying to ponder what had just happened in my mind, we passed about a dozen people that were all fishing together. As we walked by, one of them hooked a fish and I stopped to see if he was going to land it. Then another one had a fish on and then another one of them caught a fish. My wife wanted to go back to the RV and I told her to go on, that I was going to stay and learn how to catch these salmon. She headed off back to our rig, which was only a short distance away.

I stood there for a while and watched these people fish. They caught fish after fish after fish. It was obvious to me that they all knew each other as was evident from all the laughing and joking that was going on amongst them. I later found out that it was there annual family gathering.

As I have said before, I am a very shy person and in about two minutes I walked up into the middle of all those fishermen (and fisherwomen) and announced to them that I was a Cajun from south Louisiana and that I didn't know beans about how to fish salmon, that I could see that they surely knew how to fish and that I wasn't leaving until some one showed me how! I explained to them that I was raised fishing for black bass and cat fish and that I might be able to teach them a thing or two about that kind of fishing, but I was out of my league when it came to catching salmon. I neglected to tell them that my wife didn't seem to have any trouble getting a fish on her line.

There was an old gentleman there who I came to know as "Moose." I don't know what his real first name is or what his last name is. He did tell me that he had been the Tax Assessor in Anchorage for a long time and was now retired. He had been living in Alaska since the early 1950's. He took me under his wing and showed me the ropes about fishing in this Alaska river.

I had been casting out into the river and not doing very good, but he explained to me that the Sockeye Salmon followed the shore line and they were not out in the middle of the river. I had been casting for the fish in the wrong place. I was looking for them in the middle of the river and all the time they were right there under my feet. He explained to me about using a really loose drag on the reel, so the fish wouldn't break off the line every time you hooked one. I wished that he would have been around before I brought my wife down to the river. He gave me a lot of tips and even showed me the art of netting the fish after they were caught. A lot of fish are knocked off the hook at the last minute by someone trying to get the fish into a net.

I met "Moose" and some of his family down by the river for three days and each day he coached me on how to catch those elusive salmon. Finally after graduating from fishing school, I could catch salmon...**Sockeye salmon any way.** You see that in the summer time on the Kenai River the King Salmon come up the river first. Then later the Sockeye Salmon, then after them the Pink Salmon come into the river. The Pink Salmon only come into the river on even numbered years. Don't ask me how these fish know what year it is, but they do. Then at the end of the summer the Silver Salmon come into the river. You have to fish each one a little differently, but you can have a wonderful time in pursuit of each species.

I was standing on the side of the Kenai fishing for Sockeye or as the locals call them, Red Salmon, when I hooked into what I believe was a King Salmon. I never did see it, but my line started 'singing' as it was being dragged out of the reel. I tightened up the drag and the line was still being pulled out and then I tightened up the drag as tight as it would go. The line was still screaming out into the river and I was concerned that soon I would come to the end of the line and the fish would break it off. I put my thumb down hard on the line to slow it down, but I removed the thumb as soon as the skin and part of my flesh was torn off by the hot, knife like line.

Suddenly my rod snapped off! It snapped off right above the reel. I must have stood there for a second with wide opened eyes and mouth. Then I thought, 'This makes no difference. The rod can't come off the end of the line with the fish on the hook. I can still get this fish in.'

I saw my rod go down the line and disappear into the water. The line was still being pulled out and there must have been at least a hundred yards spooled off into the unknown depths of the river.

Then the thought crossed my mind that if I could tighten up the drag just a little more then I could stop the run of this fish and I could get him in. The drag on my reel was located just under the crank handle, which meant that you had to let go of the crank and reach under it to tighten or loosen the drag. I let go of the crank and as I was reaching down for the drag, my entire reel jumped off the rod handle and disappeared in the river! I stood there in disbelief holding the rod handle in my hand. My Fenwick rod was gone and my Garcia 5500C reel was gone too!

I had my photo taken holding the rod handle and spread the word along the river bank that if anyone caught a big fish with a 5500C reel attached that the reel was mine and I would like to have it back! I guess if you have to loose a rod and reel that's the best way to loose them...at least you have a good story to tell about it.

I have spent many hours fishing in Alaska and have caught a lot of fish. I am always ready to give my fellow tourist a hand and give them a few pointers on catching fish. When I show photos and video of me catching a Halibut out in Cook Inlet and they ask me how big the fish was I always say, "I didn't catch any big ones. This one was only about eighty pounds." The World Record Halibut is 459 pounds.

When you get to Alaska **do not** miss the opportunity to fish King Salmon in the Kenai River. There is nothing like dragging a fifty pound King around in the river on a string!

My first Sockeye Salmon.

My catch of Sockeye Salmon on the Kenai River in Alaska.

The little one is mine

Chapter 20: Bears

At the end of the summer we were still down on the Kenai Peninsula. The Pink Salmon were having a great run and the fishing was wonderful. We met Bill and Pat Williver, who were from Collegeville, Pennsylvania. We were camped at Morgan's Landing and we had the entire campground to ourselves. All the other campers were gone.

The fish were thick in the river and we would walk down and catch scores of fish. You could bring in a 'Pink" with almost every cast. It was great fun. Bill and I were fishing on the catch and release program and we were enjoying putting all the fish back into the river.

Early each morning Bill and I would walk down the river bank about a mile, to a good spot to fish, then some where around ten o'clock my wife would walk down and meet us. She would bring a most welcomed, thermos of hot coffee.

We walked down one morning and began to discover half eaten fish all along the trail. We made a lot of noise as we walked not wanting to surprise any bears that might have been ahead of us on the trail.

Later in the morning, June came up with the thermos of coffee. She said to us, "There were some kids trying to play a joke on me. As I walked along the trail, they were off in the weeds making a lot of noise. I believe they were trying to scare me."

159

I asked her, "How many campers are in the campground?" to which she replied, "Just two, Bill and Pat and us."

Then I asked her, "Did any of us bring any kids with us?" The answer was "No," and I asked her if she had seen the half eaten fish all along the trail. I could see in her eyes that she was putting two and two together and the answer was coming up **'BEAR!'** I knew in my heart that Bill and I were about to drink the last thermos of coffee she was going to bring us.

Bill and I started fishing closer to the campers and we didn't walk so far down the river any more.

I was fishing the Kenai with Lyle Chauvin in his boat. We had gone down the river and were anchored next to the shore trying to catch some Silver Salmon. The game warden pulled up next to us in his boat and at first, I thought that we were going to be checked for fishing licenses, but that was not the case.

He stopped his boat and asked us, "Have you seen the bear?"

"What bear?" was our joint response.

"A big, female grizzly has been harassing the fishermen along here. Probably some idiot gave the bear a few fish to eat and now she thinks that whenever she sees a boat she is supposed to get fed. The bear has tried to get into a few boats along here. Keep an eye out for her and if you see her, let me know." He bid us farewell, put his boat in gear and disappeared around a bend in the river.

I looked at Lyle and he looked at me. We both looked toward the bank of the river hoping the bear would not be there. In a few seconds Lyle said, "You know there might be a better place up the river a little ways." I immediately agreed that there had to be a better place than this to fish, so he cranked up the outboard motor and we were off. We never did see that bear and we were glad of it.

I was still camped at Morgan's Landing around the first of September. I was laying on the sofa reading, as I often did, when I noticed that a red light had come on, on the refrigerator control panel. The red light signaled that the refrigerator was not working. We were 'boon docking' with no electric hook ups, but the refrigerator would also run on propane gas. I got up and flipped all the knobs on the refrigerator and absolutely nothing happened. I tried to light a burner on the stove and it would not light.

There were two seven and a half gallon propane bottles on the front of my Coachmen travel trailer. There was a valve attached where when one bottle was empty it automatically switched to the other bottle, but I had learned from past experience that when I set the valve in this position I ended up with two empty propane bottles instead of one. I always opened one bottle and shut the other one off, that way when the first bottle became empty, I would go out and switch them over. I would turn off the empty bottle and open the full one. I would get the empty bottle refilled when I went into town.

It was around midnight and it was dark outside and chilly. I put my wind breaker on and walked over to the door and pulled the shade up. I turned the outside light on and looking out, I saw a large grizzly bear right outside of my door. When the light hit him, he stood up on his hind legs for a second and then hurriedly ran off into the dark brush.

I stood there for a minute looking through the glass window in the door. I looked over at the refrigerator and quickly determined that it wouldn't thaw out before morning. I pulled the shade down, took off the wind breaker and resumed my position on the sofa and continued my reading.

I was driving the Alaska Highway in the Yukon Territory when I noticed a large grizzly bear on the side of the road. I knew this was a great photo opportunity, so I stopped, grabbed my trusty 35mm camera, and jumped out of the Suburban. The bear was in a field about fifty yards off on the passenger side. He was just sitting there looking in my direction. He didn't look particularly menacing, so I took a few steps in his direction. I was focusing the camera and making sure everything was set like it was supposed to be when the bear moved. He turned in my direction and now sat facing me. He didn't really move closer to me. He just adjusted the way he was sitting. I guess he wanted to keep an eye on me while trying to determine if I was a threat to him.

Then it dawned on me. There was nothing between the bear and me! This bear could charge, grab me and maul me or even kill me, before I could get back inside the vehicle. These bears can run about forty miles an hour!

I snapped the picture and slowly walked back and got into the Suburban. I felt that I wasn't in danger and yet I felt that I had been in danger. In bear country you have to use your head and the thought of the good photo had clouded my judgment. I probably could have gotten just as good a picture through the window. As I have said before, the wild animals up here are *wild*. I wasn't hurt and I did get a fairly good picture, but I realized that I had put myself in danger for no apparent reason and without even giving my safety a thought.

The wilderness is a beautiful place, but sometimes it is an unforgiving and dangerous place.

We have encountered many black bears while in the Smoky Mountains of Tennessee. These bears usually have seen many people in the park and they don't seem to pay a lot of attention to you unless you have some food with you. It doesn't take one of them long to start associating people with food, after someone gives them something to eat.

We used to go to a place just north of Gatlinburg called Roaring Fork Road. The road is a part of the National Park and meanders up and down the hills along a beautiful creek that runs, sometimes roars, down the side of the mountain. We would go late in the afternoon and almost every day we would see at least one bear and sometimes more. It was not uncommon to see a big mama bear with one or two cubs. They never did seem to pose any threat to us, but we did keep our distance and most of the time viewed them from the safety of our vehicle.

We were in Cades Cove, also located in the Smoky Mountain National Park, at the picnic area. My wife's brother and sister, and some other kin folks had driven up and met us for a Smoky Mountain vacation. We had set up the Coleman stove on a picnic table and I was the chef of the day. I was cooking up some hot dogs and had a pot of hot dog chili simmering on the fire. My wife was talking to her sister.

I looked up and saw a large, black bear headed our way. He couldn't have been over twenty-five yards away when I noticed him. He had his nose in the air and was sniffing the hot dogs and chili.

I told my wife, in as calm a voice as I could muster, so no one would be alarmed, "Hey! A bear is coming!"

She looked over at me and said; "Can't you see I'm talking!" and then she went on talking to her sister again.

I said a little louder, "There is a bear.....here!"

She looked at me and glared, "I'm talking. It's very rude to interrupt!" Then she went back to talking to her sister again.

I said louder, "A bear!" It must have registered, finally, what I was trying to get across. My sister-in-law's two grandchildren were with us and a hungry black bear has been known to consider children fair game. I wanted them to put the children in the car, where they would be safe, but before I could say anything, my wife turned around and saw the bear!

"A BEAR!!!!" yelled out my wife.

'A BEAR!!!!" screamed my sister- in- law. Before anyone could say anything, they grabbed those kids and they were locked securely in the car.

I was left alone to defend the hot dogs and chili and I'll tell you right now I don't give up my hot dogs and chili easily!

I reached into my pocket and pulled out my trusty police whistle. I blew the whistle as loud as I could. The bear stopped and started to look around as though he was searching for a direction in which to escape. He put his nose back into the air and started sniffing again. The powerful smell of simmering chili on a camp stove was still drawing him to our picnic table.

I reached down on the ground and picked up a handful of pea sized gravel. The bear was about ten yard away now. I blew the whistle loudly again and threw the gravel. The rocks fell all around the bear and he took off running away from the picnic site. I usually put the whistle in my pocket when we are in bear country and I was glad that I had it with me that day. Bears don't seem to like the sound of it.

The bear ran about seventy-five yards toward another picnic site. I don't know what they had to eat at the next site, but those people decided that it was time to check out the interior of their car. The bear, meanwhile, jumped onto the table and started feasting on their lunch!

A while later, after the bear had harassed several other picnic sites, the park rangers showed up with a bear trap. *(Not a trap to catch him on the leg, a trap made out of some long barrels. The bear goes into the barrels to get some smelly bear bait and trips a device that closes the door behind him.)* It didn't take them very long to capture the animal. The last I saw of that bear, he was still in the trap and the trap had been loaded into the back end of a Park Ranger's pick up truck. He was on his way to his new home, somewhere else in the park. I know that he wasn't hungry that day, since he had eaten several nice picnic lunches.

Chapter 21: Clams

In 1992 my wife and I met Tommy and Mary Nicholson, who were originally from Vicksburg, Mississippi. We became friends and kept in touch. In the summer of 1994 they were camped in the state park near Kasilof, Alaska. We were 'boon docking' in Soldotna and drove the twenty-five miles south to meet them.

Tommy and Mary wanted us to go with them to dig for clams. Once the clams were captured, we were going to clean them and can them. It sounded like a good idea, so we agreed to go.

You have to dig for clams when the tide is low and naturally, the low tide was going to be about six-thirty in the morning! We were up early and followed behind Tommy's four wheeled drive Ford pick-up truck to the beach at Clam Gulch. We got out of our Suburban and into the back of his truck and we took off headed south on the beach.

The scenery was captivating. The blue sky was dotted with soft, white clouds. The water reflected the blueness of the sky and across the Cook Inlet the snow covered mountain peaks were standing at attention, pointed up to the heavens. Several volcanoes could be viewed across the Inlet as we drove along the sandy beach.

We took our buckets and headed down to the edge of the water. I'll give a quick lesson in how to dig clams. You walk up and down the beach and look for tiny holes in the sand. These holes are made by the clams. It you see one of these tiny holes spewing water, then you know for sure that a clam lies just a few inches below. Now a clam, and we were after Razor Clams, can dig down into the sand at a rate of about a foot a minute, so once you start to dig one up, you have to dig pretty fast.

There are several methods used to get the clams up out of the sand. Some people use a "clam gun." A clam gun is a piece of pipe about two feet long and about four inches in diameter. There is a handle bolted or welded to one end of the pipe and the handle end is closed up, except for a small quarter inch hole in the top. To work the clam gun, you first spy out where the unsuspecting clam is hiding below the sand. You put the open end of the pipe over the hole in the sand and push down on the 'gun' with all of your weight. The open end of the pipe will go down into the sand about a foot and a half. Then you put your finger over the hole in the closed in end of the gun and pull with all of your might on the handle, to pull the clam gun back up out the sand again. Putting your finger over the small hole creates a vacuum and the sand trapped inside the pipe can't get out. Take your finger off the hole in the top and bang the clam gun on the beach and all the sand that you have trapped in the gun will come out, and hopefully, the clam will fall out too. You can just pick him up and put him into your bucket.

Another method of gathering clams is with the clam shovel. The clam shovel works just like the common garden variety shovel, but the clam shovel is long and narrow, being only about five or six inches wide and about eighteen inches long. The blade of the shovel has a distinctive curve made into it, so when you push the shovel down into the sand, the blade, optimistically, will go under the fast digging clam and bring him up.

I prefer the old fashion method. Get down and dirty on the beach. You have to be willing to get wet and to get full of sand, but those clams are under the sand and you are on top of the sand. The challenge is on…..man against clam!

When you have decided where the clam is located, then you just start to dig down with your hands and fingers. You can dig pretty fast into the wet sand and after some quick excavating; you can feel the top of the clam's shell. You can feel the shell moving as the clam is digging down as fast as he can. Just hold onto the clam and pull him up! **Nothing to it!**

After digging up several dozen clams by hand and looking at my bleeding fingers, I learned why they call them **"Razor"** Clams. Maybe next time, I might opt for a thin pair of gloves.

We took our catch and drove back to Johnson Lake Park where the Nicholsons were camped in their fifth wheel trailer. Tommy and Mary were old hands at canning and quickly had all of their equipment set up and then the real work began. We steamed the clams open and took them out of their shells. Then they had to be cleaned and cut up, or as we were doing it, ground up in a hand grinder. Then Tommy and Mary cooked the clams and sealed them into tin cans, just like the ones you buy from the store. The cans were cooked in a pressure cooker for a while and then put into cold water the second they were done, to ensure they were properly sealed. Then they were ready to store, or you could open one up and get the clam chowder going!

This sounds easy, but the cleaning and the cooking and the canning really takes up a lot of time and after hours and hours of work, we were finally finished.

I told Tommy and Mary that I was ready to go claming whenever they were. I let them know, that after I caught my share of clams and put them into my trusty clam bucket, they were welcomed to have them and I was going home. You can buy clams at the grocery store for a buck a can and that was sure a lot easier than canning them yourself, even if they didn't taste quite as good.

The Nicholsons at Exit Glacier, Alaska

Chapter 22: Volcano

At the end of August, 1992, we were still at Morgan's Landing just east of Soldotna, Alaska. We were watching the news on TV and the announcer started telling about a volcano eruption in Alaska. It was one of those times when we were not really paying much attention and just got the tail end of what was being said.

We didn't know where the volcano was located. We hadn't heard that part of the news broadcast. I brushed it off and told my wife that it was probably down on the Aleutian Chain some place and surely it wouldn't affect us.

No one in the campground seemed to be paying any attention to anything, other than where the fish were running and who was catching what, etc.

The weather was good and the sun was shining and we didn't have a lot of concern about the volcano. I mentioned to my wife that I sure would like to see the volcano while it was erupting.....from a distance, of course.

What we did not know, was that Mount Spur had erupted just to the north and across the Cook Inlet from us! I could have gotten into my suburban and driven about ten or fifteen miles and had a really good view of the whole event, but not knowing lot about the area, I had no idea where Mount Spur was located.

We kept hearing the reports on TV, and really, we still didn't pay a lot of attention. Then the news reports began coming in that a cloud of ash had fallen on Anchorage! Anchorage was about one hundred and fifty miles away by road, but probably less than half that by air! Now our concern was a little greater, since a shift in the wind would evidently bring that ash cloud down on top of us!

The wind did not shift, however, and the volcano quieted down and started to behave and the scientist began to give the all clear, so to speak.

A few days later we pulled into Anchorage. We were on our way to the Alaska State Fair, which is held in Palmer, every Labor Day weekend. We started to see the volcano 'signs' around Portage. The glaciers that can be seen from the highway had all been covered in a layer of brown. We remarked that in the future you would probably be able to see exactly where the glacier ice was on the day of the eruption, because there would be this layer of brown ash wedged in between the layers of ice.

We drove into Anchorage and the entire city was colored in brown! The volcanic ash was every where. Men were on the roof of the Sears store shoveling up the ash by the wheel barrow full and throwing it down into the parking lot. The ash must have been a foot deep up there, seeing how much of the brown, volcanic material that had been removed from the roof.

The ash was every where. The streets were brown, the lawns were brown and a lot of the cars and trucks were coated in a brown film!

The TV news advised everyone to change the air filters on the engines of their vehicles and seeing all the ash and the dust that resulted from it, I thought that this was a good idea. We had heard that the ash was very abrasive and if it got into your engine could cause some serious damage, so we decided to get a couple of air filters for our Suburban.

After checking a number of auto parts stores, we started to understand that we were not the only ones that thought changing air filters was a good idea. It was easier to find gold in Anchorage than it was to find an air filter for your car!

It wasn't but just a few minutes after the ash started to fall on Anchorage, that all the souvenir shops started selling 'I SURVIVED THE VOLCANO' Tee shirts and bumper stickers. Booths started to appear in all the malls selling little, plastic bottles of volcanic ash and it wasn't cheap either. I filled up my own little, plastic bottle with ash from the Sear's parking lot!

We were back in Anchorage in 1994 and there was really no visible evidence that the city had ever been covered with volcanic ash. Trees and lawns were green again. All the streets and parking lots were clean and the ice in the glaciers was colored a nice blue and white, as in past times. Nature does have a way of cleaning up her own act.

Chapter 23: Earthquakes

We have spent several summers and winters in Alaska. What can I say? We like it!

During our first winter in Alaska, we were camped at the Golden Nugget RV Park in Anchorage. *(Yes, you can camp in Alaska in the winter. I'll tell you all about it in the next chapter.)* Our travel trailer had a front bedroom and my wife was in the bedroom watching TV. I was in the living room watching TV. We like to watch different programs together and the door was closed between the bedroom and the living room.

I felt, what seemed to me, as though some huge man with a twelve pound sledge hammer had just taken a swing with all of his might and hit the tip end of the trailer hitch. The entire trailer vibrated as though being struck a blow!

I thought that maybe my wife had dropped something, although I couldn't think of anything in the bedroom that would have been heavy enough to make all that racket, unless the TV had fallen off the shelf. I jumped up and opened the door to find my wife standing on the other side, her mouth and eyes wide open. We had experienced our first earthquake, or probably our first good earth tremor. We had never been in anything like it before and it was over with before we knew what was happening. The TV nightly news confirmed that we had indeed felt the earth move and that no damage had been reported.

I had always been curious about earthquakes, even as a child. I remember my Grandfather telling me that he was in an earthquake once. To him it felt as though a big truck had passed by and shook the ground.

One year while we were in the mountains of Tennessee, the news reported that a minor earthquake had occurred. I hadn't felt anything that day and I was disappointed. I didn't want to be in some tremendous, damage causing quake, I just wanted to be able to say that I had experienced one. Well, now I could say that, but my experiences were not over yet.

We had parked the Coachmen travel trailer at the Eagle River State Park, just north of Anchorage. It is a beautiful park with paved sites and fire rings, but of course there are no hook ups, so we were 'boon docking' again.

We drove around the campground and found a nice place and I backed the trailer into position. I got out of the Suburban to check things out. I had backed the camper parallel to the Eagle River. The Eagle River was about ten feet straight out of my front door..... and about a hundred feet straight down! I remarked to my wife that I didn't know if I wanted to stay on this spot. When she asked me why, I told her I didn't want to be on the side of that cliff if another earthquake came along. She actually thought I was joking, but I really wasn't. She laughed at me and so I just went on setting the leveling jacks down and making sure everything was as it was supposed to be.

We were having a lot of fun eating Chinese buffets in town and sitting around the campfires we made each night. We had slept peacefully every one of the four nights we had been in the park. We went to bed as usual on the fifth night.

At 3:05 AM we were rudely awakened by being almost thrown out of our bed. Everything was being violently shaken and moved around and although we quickly jumped out of bed we were disoriented. We were staggering around as if we were drunk. We couldn't move like we wanted to. We were in 5.7 earthquake that shook us and shook us for a full thirty seconds!

The shaking stopped as suddenly as it had started. I walked to the window and pulled the shade up and turned on the outside light. I opened the door and estimated the distance to the edge of the pavement on the campsite. I couldn't see where the camper had moved any closer to the edge and I don't mind telling you that I was greatly relieved. I won't tell you what pictures went through my mind of our travel trailer hanging off the side of that cliff.

The earthquake being over, my wife promptly went back to bed and in a few minutes was sound asleep again. I lay in the bed, but I was in no mood to go back to sleep. My desire to be in an earthquake had been fulfilled and I had quickly decided that it was not something I wanted to try again. I could find no damage to anything upon a quick inspection before I returned to bed, but we were still perched up on that cliff. There were some small trees growing between me and the river, but they were *small* trees. I lay there and thanked the Lord that we were safe and tried to go back to sleep.

At 3:25 AM I was still awake. I heard a sound as of heavy iron being bent and twisted and rubbed together. I didn't have time to try to determine what the sound was, because the trailer started shaking violently again! This time it went on for about fifteen or twenty seconds. It didn't shake as badly the second time as it had the first, but it shook plenty enough for me! As soon as the shaking stopped, I jumped up and immediately headed for the door to make sure the trailer was still where it was supposed to be. Thank the Lord again...it was!

My wife and I couldn't find any visible damage and soon she was back in bed asleep, while I lay there keeping guard, although I still don't know how to guard against an earthquake.

There was some minor damage reported in the area and we heard all about it on the TV news broadcast the next day.

Outside my camper door I could see two large, highway bridges that cross the Eagle River. I sat there the next morning drinking coffee and watching a lot of big trailer trucks going to and fro across the bridges. I guessed that the bridges were OK and I was glad that I wasn't the first one to have to cross over one of them after the ground stopped shaking.

I was in the Anchorage Airport on a sunny Sunday Morning. I was in the place where they check you out before you are allowed to get on the airplane. All of a sudden the walk through metal detectors started screaming their alarms. There were just a few people in the room and everyone was just sort of frozen in place. Then everything started shaking! The floor of the terminal appeared to have waves going down the hallway. The ceiling also looked like ocean waves flowing along it. Then in a few seconds it stopped! Then it seemed as if everyone in the room took in a breath at the same time. Everyone started talking at once and then in about another minute the metal detectors started singing again! The whole place shook and shook and then as suddenly as it had started, it stopped. Some of the passengers turned around and headed back out of the exit. There seemed to be no damage from the shaking and it was soon business as usual at the airport.

As far as I'm concerned, I know as much as I need to know about being in an earthquake. My curiosity has been greatly satisfied.....several times!

Chapter 24: Winter Camping in Alaska

Yes, you can camp in Alaska in the winter! You may well ask, "How?" Well, you can't just pull up into a campground and get out and hook up your water and electric and sewer hose and start camping when the temperature is twenty below zero, but you can stay the winter in Alaska in your RV if you have prepared well. We have stayed five winters in Anchorage and have had only very minor problems.

Our first winter was the winter of '94 which was one of the snowiest winters on record for the Anchorage area. We stayed in our travel trailer when the mercury would only come 'up' to twenty below!

We learned that there are several campgrounds that do stay open all winter. We determined to go to Anchorage where there are more malls and grocery stores, more things to do, during the long northern winter. We made reservations at the Golden Nugget RV Park in Anchorage and pulled in, in October, determined to become Sourdoughs! (*A Sourdough is supposedly someone who is in Alaska when things freeze up....and is still there at breakup, or when things thaw out again.*) We had heard that summer in Alaska was for the tourists and winter was for the real Alaskans and we wanted to know why the people who lived in 'The Great Land' kept telling us this.

I registered at the office and paid my first month's rent and I asked the girl to tell me exactly what to do to prepare for the winter. I had heard a lot of advice from a lot of people who had never stayed over in the winter and I didn't want any below zero surprises, if I could prevent them. She referred me to a man named Bob, who had spent several winters at the Golden Nugget.

Bob and his wife, Sara were very pleasant and friendly folks and Bob couldn't wait to advise me on what to do. Bob and Sara had spent several winters in Anchorage, in their fifth wheel travel trailer. He told me that he had had no major problems. I decided that I was going to do what he said to do. I wanted to be prepared for whatever the winter would bring us and I wanted to do the preparation correctly. My wife and I, up until this time, thought winter consisted of about six or seven days of temperatures in the high thirty's. Winter in south Louisiana is not really a big threat, but up here it would be a totally different story. I tried to follow Bob's expert advice in detail.

First, I went down to the friendly Wal Mart store and purchased some heat strips for the water and sewer hoses. Heat strips are electric wires that generate heat to prevent your water lines from freezing up and they work on 110 volt electric current. I measured my water hose and cut it to the shortest length that would fit between the RV water connection and the water faucet. I dug a hole about two and a half feet deep down around the water pipe that was supplying us with water. I started wrapping the heat strip from this point and wrapped it around my faucet and my water hose all the way to the water connection on the RV. Then I wrapped the whole thing in a blanket of pipe insulation, over which I wrapped a plastic covering that came with the insulation. Over all this I placed some plastic, foam pipe insulators and taped the whole thing from start to finish with trusty duct tape. *(I understand that you are supposed to always have a good supply of duct tape when you are in Alaska.)* Now that my water hose was about three inches thick with insulation and heat strip, I felt secure and did the same thing with my sewer hose. During my last couple of winters I found some foam rubber insulation that went directly over the water hose and heat strip without having to put all the insulation wrap, plastic covering, etc. and it worked great without a fraction of the work.

The next thing I did was to skirt the camper. The first year, I cut and placed quarter inch plywood all around with R21 insulation stapled to the side of the plywood that went under the trailer. The second winter, I found out that one inch Styrofoam sheets were a lot easier cut and fit better, with a lot less trouble and work and it was a lot cheaper too!

With the camper skirted, I had a place to store some of the things I had been carrying around in my "shed"….. the back end of my Suburban. You know all the things that you accumulate and haul around with you when you travel, like my step ladder *(All full timers have a step ladder!)* and my plastic gas cans for the generator. I emptied and rinsed them out, of course. I stored some other things under the trailer, like the regular (summer) tires that went on the back of the Suburban, our lawn chairs and folding tables, and then my wife sealed the whole thing up with spray foam sealer. I had built a sliding door out of plywood and a one inch thick piece of Styrofoam sheet and placed it so I could get to the gray water and black water valves on the sewer system of the trailer, if I had to.

I plugged in a 100 watt light bulb and put it under the camper, through the door I had built to access the sewer valves, to keep the air under the camper and the near the sewer valves warmer. Later when we camped in our Bounder motor home I placed a couple of 100 watt light bulbs in the compartment where all the sewer and water hoses and electric connections go into the motor home. I bought a 'remote control' thermometer so that I could see the temperature in the outside box from inside my living room in the RV. The device would 'beep' when the temp fell below about 35 degrees so that I could check it out and usually change a light bulb. I also put a 100 watt light bulb inside of one of our outside storage compartments and we kept our liquid laundry detergent, spare spray cans of whatever and anything that we thought couldn't stand the freeze. I had a temperature sensor in this box also. This worked great and we didn't have any problems with it at all. It was a great comfort to be able to look at the gauge and see what the temperature was n those outside boxes without having to go out there and check around every day.

I also took a seventy-five watt light bulb and made a light socket that would fit into the outside service area of the refrigerator. The refrigerator works by a heat source, either electric or propane, heating up the tube with the refrigerant gasses in it. This causes the gasses to circulate through the system and cools the refrigerator. When the temperature goes below zero, sometimes this system doesn't generate enough heat to heat up this tube, so the refrigerator won't work. Bob told me that when the temperature is thirty below zero outside that your ice cream could melt in your freezer. *(I didn't know if I would want any ice cream when the temperature was thirty below zero.)* He said the light bulb would keep the refrigerator compartment warm and the refrigerator would work perfectly.

I also made a wooden box to fit over the water faucet, insulated it with R21 insulation and put a seventy-five watt light bulb inside the box to keep the hose connection to the faucet as warm and cozy as possible.

We bought some plastic film to put over the inside of the windows. This plastic film comes with some two sided tape that you stick all around the edges of the windows and then the sheet of plastic is cut to fit and stuck to the tape also. The plastic film is then heated with a hair dryer and it shrinks up for a good, tight fit and you can see right through it almost as good as through the window glass. Doing this puts about a half inch space between the window glass and the plastic film and will prevent your heat from being drained outside the RV through the glass. In the Bounder motor home we have double paned windows so we only used the plastic on the single paned door glass and also we put some plastic sheeting on the inside of the windshields.

I also took some Styrofoam insulation and insulated the 'inside' of our 'outside' storage boxes on the trailer. The outside boxes actually opened up into the 'inside' of the trailer. One of the 'outside' storage boxes was in reality, storage under the bed and the other one was storage under the closet in the bathroom.

My wife and I put in three or four days of hard work getting everything ready. Having done all this we waited for the really cold weather. It didn't take long. It started snowing on October 14th and by the morning of the 15th we had about ten inches of snow on the ground! We loved it! Having never been in snow before, we thought it was a beautifully, wondrous thing!

That was the day we were introduced to the **snow shovel**. We had never seen one before and Bob had told us to get one. We had a pretty orange one with a wooden handle.

I shoveled the snow up against the skirting on the RV. Bob said it was a good insulator and would hold the heat under the camper. I couldn't figure out, in my south Louisiana mind, how cold snow could keep in the heat, but I knew it would, because Bob told me it would.

I also had to shovel the driveway. The campground had a snow plow and they quickly and efficiently kept the streets cleared of the snow. The driveway was my responsibility. I got out my trusty, orange snow shovel and went to work. My wife kept nagging and nagging me, because she wanted to shovel the snow, but I was in command and I shoveled and shoveled until my back told me that I should give in and let her have a turn too. By the end of the second week, neither of us wanted to even see that shovel!

If there are any drawbacks to staying in Alaska in the winter, they are snow shoveling and scraping the ice off the windshield. Other than these two chores that have to be performed, we love Alaska winter!

While in the Bounder motor home we towed a Saturn car. When winter came upon us I had the Best Buy store install a remote control starter in the little Saturn. I would leave the heater on 'wide open' and about ten minutes before time to leave I would press the two buttons on the remote control starter that was hanging from my key ring and the Saturn would crank up. In ten minutes the car was warm and any snow and ice on the windshield was melted or quickly disposed of with the windshield wipers!

And one other thing about camping in sub zero weather. As I have said before, we had a front bed room in our trailer. The bed was cross wise across the very front end of the trailer. I guess the insulation in the front wall of the trailer was a little lacking, because on really cold nights the blanket would freeze to the front wall! The furnace and electric heaters kept the trailer nice and cozy, but I guess the heat just didn't quite make it all the way to that front wall.

One morning I got up and started to run some water in the kitchen sink. I turned on the hot water faucet and nothing came out! The hot water pipe was frozen! I told myself that I wasn't going to panic and tried to think of what I was going to do. Pictures of us going off to the bath house in the cold for the rest of the winter flashed through my mind. The cold water was working fine and I was grateful for that.

I got out the hair dryer. I turned it up as hot as it would go and I started heating up the pipes. You could see most of the water pipes as they ran along the walls under the dinette and in the bottom of cabinets. In a few places you had to take some drawers out and move some things around, but you could see the pipes running close to the inside wall. I left the hot water open at the kitchen sink. The sink was the end of the water line. As I heated a curve in the pipe hidden in what was really the rear outside compartment, the water started flowing through the faucet.

This happened about four or five times and after the first few times; I knew where to heat the pipe. The RV Park (and Bob) recommended that we always let the water drip when the temperature went below about twenty degrees and I'm sure that this helped keep the water flowing all winter.

We had a wonderful time during those winters. We learned to cross country ski and to ice skate. I learned how to cut a hole in the ice and fish. I rode a dog sled, saw the start of the Iditarod sled dog races and we spent a lot of time site seeing. *(Yes you can site see in Alaska in the winter!)*

Fur Rendezvous is a big winter festival held in Anchorage. There is a big fireworks show to kick things off and a parade marches through the down town area the next day. I have seen thousands of people out along the parade route when the temperature was ten degrees!

There is a carnival or as we would say in Louisiana, a street fair, during the Fur Rondy. You get a chance to ride the Ferris wheel in single degree temps! There are car races…..that's what I said…car races and dog sled races and probably a few other kinds of races, if you will look around. There are many arts and crafts shows that take place at this time and we have thoroughly enjoyed the Rendezvous every time we have attended.

All of the roads in Alaska are kept open all winter and we did a lot of traveling with no problems what ever. In the early part of October, we changed the rear tires on our Suburban over to studded winter tires. These are cold weather tires with what looks like a lot of small metal nails protruding from the tread. They are designed to run on ice and they do a superb job. We didn't have four wheel drive on our vehicle and we did not have any trouble at all driving around in the snow and ice. Of course we were careful and tried not to do anything stupid while we were driving. We had an engine block heater installed on the Suburban, to prevent any engine freezing problems while the vehicle was parked during those cold, cold nights.

It was a common thing for us to drive the forty miles to Alyeska Ski Resort or the fifty miles to Portage Glacier. We even drove the one hundred and sixty miles down to Soldotna and Kenai a few times.

Of course when we did travel, we always had blankets and extra clothing in the back of our Suburban and we always carried our trusty Coleman stove and an ample supply of propane, just in case.

My wife and I had a great time winter camping in the far north. It doesn't really stay dark all winter, unless you are up in Barrow on the Arctic Ocean. The shortest day in Anchorage is about five and a half hours. It is kind of neat the way the sun comes up in the south, hangs there about eye level and then sets in the south too.

The Northern Lights are marvelous and we saw them often. A lot of tourists go up in the summer and don't get a chance to see the lights. *(It doesn't get dark at night in the summer.)* If you are looking for a good reason to travel to Alaska in the winter, the Aurora Borealis is a wonderful reason. I have to admit that the first time I walked outside and the sky was bright green and yellow it did give me a strange, eerie feeling. It looked to me like something you would see in a science fiction movie.

One drawback to wintering in Alaska is the price of produce at the supermarket. I went to a large supermarket in Anchorage and saw that the Iceberg Lettuce was $2.98 a pound! I didn't buy any, but I thought of bringing my camera and taking a picture of that sign.

So you CAN camp in Alaska in the cold weather and you CAN enjoy it. If you think the scenery is beautiful up there in the summer time, then you should see it in the winter! I believe that Alaska in the winter time looks like Alaska is supposed to look. We loved it!

A little snow in Alaska.

Chapter 25: Two Southward Bound Trips

I want to tell about **_two different trips_** that we took when we left Alaska and headed south. The first time we left Alaska was in September of 1994 and we towed our travel trailer with us. This was an early fall trip. The second southbound trip I want to tell you about took place in March of 1996. This trip started out in spring and soon turned into winter. We had traded in our travel trailer and drove out in our Suburban.

Trip Number One (Fall)

At the end of our first Alaska summer in 1992, we were still towing our Coachmen trailer. We drove down the Alaska Highway in September. We intended to go all the way to Dawson Creek on the Al-Can and then down into Washington State. We stopped at Campground Services in Watson Lake, Yukon Territory and since our camper was full of mud, we decided to wash it. There was a coin operated, pressure washer in the campground.

I put some coins in and started to get the mud off the trailer. My wife came over and said that she wanted to wash the trailer so I gave her the pressure washer and I went off checking on the trailer hook up, engine, etc. I walked back around to where she was washing the trailer and I noticed right away that she had washed off a portion of the striping on the side of the camper! This greatly upset me, but being the loving husband that I am, I soon got over it and we have had many a good laugh about the time she washed the stripes right off the camper. It was one of those things that are really funny now, but it wasn't so funny then.

While in the campground in Watson Lake, a man told me that he had just come up the Cassiar Highway and that it was all paved, except for about twenty miles of gravel. We had not previously traveled this road and since it probably would have been a little short-cut we decided to take this route.

We left Watson Lake and headed south on the Cassiar Highway. We hadn't gone but about twenty miles when it started to rain. It was STILL raining when we reached the end of it, about 375 miles later. Our Suburban was white and our trailer was white and blue, but you couldn't tell what color they were by the time we got back on paved roads. They were entirely covered with a sheet of mud! That guy was right; there was only about twenty miles of gravel. He didn't tell me about the seventy miles of mud! We did learn a lesson, though. Only believe that the gravel roads up in the North Country have been paved if you see it with your own eyes!

The scenery on the Cassiar Highway was grand. I would like to travel that road again someday.....in the sunshine!

I pulled up into a truck wash to get the mud off the truck and trailer. I was very careful and just washed the mud *(and not the stripes)* off the RV!

We pulled up into Stewart, British Columbia and spent the night parked at the Bear Glacier. You could sit at our table and the glacier was right outside the window. It was a very pleasant experience camping there. The cold air coming off that glacier sure made us enjoy our quilts that night.

Several months later I was having the oil changed in a Sears service center in San Jose, California. The mechanic walked over and asked, "Where in the world have you been in that truck. There is mud about three inches thick under there!

At least when the trailer was full of mud you couldn't see where my wife had washed the stripes off.

We drove through Washington State and stopped in Dallas, Oregon again, to visit our oldest son, Emmitt David. About the second week in October, we pulled over to the coast and started driving south on Highway 101, the famous Coast Highway.

It is a lovely drive with the exquisite Pacific Ocean right outside the window for hundreds of miles. We drove through pretty towns with names like Depoe Bay, Florence, Port Orford and Gold Beach. We crossed the border into California and passed through Crescent City. We stopped in the National Park

Orick, where you can park your rig right on the beach. Intending to stay for one night, we finally left four days later. The whales were playing right near the shore and after four days of watching them, my eye sockets were sore from pressing the binoculars against them.

We went on south through Eureka and Rio Dell. We got off Highway 101 at Leggett and started down Highway 1, headed toward Los Angeles.

We were taking our time and seeing the sites as we went along. We had no time schedule to follow and we were enjoying the ride and the scenery tremendously.

We drove down the Avenue of Giants and admired all the huge Redwood trees. We stopped and toured the "One Log" house and poked around in all the gift shops. We continued southward, crossed the Golden Gate Bridge and stopped in San Francisco.

We went out to Alcatraz and did our 'time on the rock,' explored Fisherman's Wharf, climbed aboard all the old, sailing ships at the Maritime Museum and took pictures of all the sea lions that had taken over the yacht harbor.

We walked the Board Walk at Santa Cruz, saw Cannery Row in Monterrey and ate at the Hog's Breath Inn, owned by Clint Eastwood, in Carmel By the Sea.

We stopped at the Hurst Castle in San Simeon. It was very impressive, but I thought that this guy, Hurst, sure knew how to waste a lot, and I do mean a *"lot"*, of money!

Farther south we went. Through San Luis Obispo and into the quaint towns of Solvang, a Danish looking place comple with windmills and Santa Yenez, which looks like an old cowbo town. We stopped and camped at the Rancho Oso RV Par which is near Santa Barbara.

We were sitting outside of our trailer late in the afternoo We had been site seeing all day in Santa Barbara and we wer relaxing and enjoying a soft drink. The wind started to pick u and in no time was blowing about fifty or sixty miles an hou The sky was clear and there were no clouds or signs o approaching bad weather, only this wind that seemed to ge stronger by the minute. We didn't know what to expect. Th other people in the campground seemed to pay the wind n attention and went about their normal camping business. W were experiencing our first "Santa Anna" winds, or as I hear one man refer to them our first "Sundowner."

I'm no weather man, so I can't explain what causes this wind but it is something to do with the heat off the land and the coo breezes from the ocean coming together. I might be totall wrong in this explanation, but that's how it was explained to me.

Well, about ten o'clock PM, those winds diminished and soo all was calm. The next day late in the afternoon the winds picke up again and in a short while a full gale was blowing. This time with a little knowledge of what was going on, we just retired int the trailer and closed all the windows to try to keep the dust from blowing in.

On southward we ventured. We stopped in Ventura and drove down and walked the famous streets of Hollywood and took a tour of the homes of the stars. We saw all the hand and foot prints at the Chinese Theater and spent an enjoyable and exciting day at Universal Studios.

After pulling into Anaheim and getting the rig tucked into our site at the Anaheim Harbor RV Park, we visited the Crystal Cathedral. Boy, I sure wouldn't want to have to wash all those windows!

The next day, one of my boyhood dreams came true! **We went to Disneyland!** We had gone to Disney World in Florida a number of times, but my memory went back to 1955. I remembered seeing Davy Crockett (Fess Parker) and his side kick, (Buddy Ebson) riding up to officially open Disneyland, on our black and white TV set. I made up my mind that one day I was going to go there and see that place in person and here we were! It had only taken me thirty-seven years, but I finally made it.

Speaking of childhood dreams, since we have retired a lot of the things we had only dreamed about, have come true. I believe that a person can pursue his dream, no matter what the dream is, or he can just sit at home and suppress that dream. It doesn't matter how old the dream is, or how many years the dream has been subdued.   In reality, the choice is yours. You have to determine...to make the decision...that your dream WILL come true!

My wife and I spent a very enjoyable day aboard the Queen Mary. The Queen Mary is docked in Long Beach and is open to the public for tours.

We were sitting in one of the restaurants having coffee when we heard one of the waitresses telling a story about a ghost that visits the restaurant. For those of you that don't know, the Queen Mary is famous for a lot of ghosts that are supposed to be wandering around the ship. Anyway, she was telling about a woman that often comes into the restaurant and sits down at a certain table and orders coffee. When the waitress goes to get the coffee, she disappears! Then the waitress said, "She always sits at the same table and in the same chair. She sits in that chair," and saying this she pointed to the chair I was sitting in!

There are other stories of hearing screams and voices coming out of the 'Forecastle' where a number of German prisoners of war died. There is a dancer that some people see dancing in the ball room. There is also another story of a ghost mechanic that inhabits the engine room. We didn't see any ghosts on our visit. *(But it sure was spooky down in that engine room!)*

We headed back north on I-15 and visited the Roy Rogers and Dale Evans museum and then headed out of California and nto Nevada. We pulled into the Hacienda RV Park and my electric jack on the trailer broke again. I took that jack and put it n the trash dumpster where it belonged.

We saw the lights on the "Strip," lost a little money in the casinos and ate a lot of low priced buffets. Some friends of ours from Tennessee flew out and met us and we had a great time visiting with them and seeing the sites. We drove down to Hoover Dam, took the tour and then took the long way back to Las Vegas through the desert.

In the meantime our youngest son, Randy, Jr. had moved to San Jose, so when we got through spending our money in Las Vegas, we were headed back west to spend some time with him.

After our visit we headed back eastward and saw the London Bridge at Lake Havasu City and then drove down to Quartsite, Arizona. It was February 1993 and the giant flea market was in progress. We purchased a camping pass from the Bureau of Land Management (BLM), drove down the road until we found a good spot, pulled off into the desert and started camping. We were 'boon docking' again with no hook ups, but I had bought a small generator and the BLM pass allowed us to dump our tanks and fill up with fresh water anytime we wanted to..

We went down to the flea marked and walked it for eight days in a row. We didn't see all of it and determined that we would come back another time and see it all. *(We did just that in 1994.)*

The flea market is a very interesting place. We saw everything for sale from false teeth to airplanes! It is the only place that I know of where you can buy dinosaur bones and other fossils in museum quality condition. There are more types of crafts than you can shake a stick at and one whole week is a RV show, with all kinds of gadgets and toys to buy for your rig. You can purchase RVs that range from "pop up' trailers to forty foot motor home.

We left Quartsite and headed east on I-10, back to Louisiana to visit family. We did make a few stops on the way.

We looked all around the Saguaro Monument Park and spent a day in Old Tucson, where about ten thousand cowboy movies were filmed. I've seen so many westerns that were filmed here, that I thought I had been there before.

We stopped in Tombstone and saw the original OK Corral It's still there and doesn't look like what they usually show in the movies. We went down to Bisbee and took the train into the mountain to see the Queen Mine.

The mine trip is a good one. The only lights inside the mine or the headlights that are issued to the tour members, so you get a feel of what it was like to work down, deep in the earth with only the light and battery that you bring with you.

We stopped at the Alamo in San Antonio and drove over to Brackettville to see the Alamo that John Wayne built for the movie. The set was also used for the just released version of the Alamo.

We drove on into Louisiana and visited friends and family and then decided to head back north, but this time we decided to explore the east coast and go up into New England and on into the Maritime Provinces of Canada, but first I wanted to go to the Dulcimer conference in Mountain View, Arkansas.

I learned a few new things about playing the Dulcimer and after thoroughly enjoying being in the Ozark Mountains; we headed to Tennessee on our way to the east coast and on to New England.

At home in the desert at Quartzsite, Arizona

Trip Number Two (Spring that turns into Winter)

We left Alaska in late March of 1996 after purchasing a Bounder motor home and deciding to save shipping charges and pick it up in California. The way motor homes are delivered from the factory is a simple method. Someone gets in and drives them up. We had seen motor homes on their way to being delivered while driving the Alaska Highway. Some of them were even towing large travel trailers behind them, which were being delivered to the dealers also. I'm not criticizing the way this is done and I'm sure it is the fastest and most economical way to do it, but June and I decided that we would rather have our new motor home without the four thousand miles of hard driving put on it by the delivery team.

We traded in our travel trailer at A&M RV Center in Anchorage. We believed that we had made a good deal, and the only drawback was that our motor home was to be built in Riverside, California and that was about four thousand miles away!

We sold a lot of our "stuff" at least the "stuff" we found hidden away in the trailer that we hadn't seen in a few years, gave away some things and packed the rest in boxes that we loaded into the back end of the Suburban. As Bob, our neighbor said on the morning we left, "We couldn't get a sardine in the back of the Suburban if we tried." We had some of our "stuff" loaded in boxes and the boxes wouldn't fit into the back end of the vehicle because it was packed so full. I went to Sears and bought one of those adjustable racks that attaches to the roof top of the vehicle. We put our 'extra' boxes into some large plastic garbage bags, taped them up with trusty duct tape and strapped them to the top of the truck. The back seat and back floor were also full of our treasures. We even had things on the front seat between us.

It was March 30 and the temperature in Anchorage was about forty-five degrees. The streets were all thawed out. Breakup was here and we were off on another great adventure. We were, I guess, in the strictest sense, 'homeless'. The dealer in Anchorage had our traded in trailer and the dealer in California had our Bounder and it was about four thousand miles between the two.

We took off in bright sunshine and drove over four hundred miles to Beaver Creek, Yukon Territory, only having to stop and adjust the straps on the roof rack about half a dozen times until I discovered I had put the strap buckles on backwards and solved the problem. We crossed the border into Canada without any problems, although I admit that we prayed that the border guards wouldn't make us unpack all those boxes!

We stopped at a motel and I asked the lady at the desk how cold it had been at night. She told me that it was about as cold as it was right then. She had a big thermometer outside her office door and on the way out I checked the temp and it was about twenty-five degrees. I didn't plug in the engine block heater as I thought of doing. We were tired and we went on to bed.

The next morning, I was out loading all the things back into the Suburban that we had taken into the room with us. It felt colder to me than the twenty-five degrees had felt the night before and I walked to the office and looked at the thermometer. It was forty degrees below zero!

I got into our Suburban and the engine cranked right up. I was glad about that, but I looked at the oil pressure gauge and it read ZERO! I let the engine run for about two minutes and still no pressure. I switched the engine off and hoped that whatever oil was in the engine had heated up and would drain down into the oil pan and heat up the rest of the engine oil. I had always added 'Slick 50' additive to our engine oil since the Suburban was building up quite a lot of miles on her and now was a good opportunity to see if it was as good as they said it was. I waited for a couple of minutes and I cranked up the engine again. There still wasn't any oil pressure, but I just let the engine run, making sure not to touch the accelerator. I looked at my watch and just sat there waiting for the engine to warm up. Twelve minutes later the oil pressure had come up to normal.

I don't know if I handled this correctly. The old timers used to build fires under their engines to thaw them out, but that was when they couldn't get them to start. It didn't seem to harm anything as we drove the Suburban all the way to southern California and then to Las Vegas where we traded 'Old Herbie,' as we called the Suburban, off on a new Saturn that we could tow behind the motor home. At that time the Suburban had 177,000 miles on it and we had made no repairs to the engine, except for plug wires and two fuel pumps. We had seen to it that we did the scheduled oil changes and we changed the belts and distributor caps about every fifty thousand miles or so. We really got our moneys worth from that vehicle and because of this we made sure that our Bounder was built with a Chevrolet engine.

Since we are talking about winter up in the high north, let me tell you about what we saw on the Alaska Highway, just south of Beaver Creek. We had stopped at a road construction site and were waiting for a 'Pilot Truck' to guide us through. The lady stopping the traffic told us that it was *forty-five below zero*.

Just as the 'Pilot Truck' came up, the water truck came up also. At road construction sites, it is a common thing to see the water truck wetting the road to keep the dust down, but it was, as I have said before, FORTY-FIVE BELOW ZERO!

There was steam coming up from the back of the water truck and a heavy smell of sulfur. I guess he had filled up the tank on the truck from a hot spring located somewhere in the area.

He pulled up in the front of the 'Pilot Truck' and opened his valve and began to dump water onto the road way. It came out of the pipe on the back of his truck as water, but by the time the water hit the roadbed it had turned to ice and just bounced around all over the gravel! *Talk about government jobs!*

We drove over that bed of ice cubes until the truck ran out of water. He then pulled over and we proceeded behind the 'Pilot Truck' until we came to the end of the construction.

We drove the Alaska Highway when it was snowing so hard that we had to stop because we couldn't see out of the windshield. We sat there and prayed that no one would drive into the rear end of us. In a few minutes the white-out lifted and we were on our way again.

We came to a place where an avalanche had covered about a mile of the highway with snow, rocks and broken and battered trees. When we arrived the road had just been opened again by the highway crew and their company of bull dozers. There was snow and broken trees stacked twenty feet high on the sides of the roadway.

We had not realized that it would still be winter in the interior of the country, when the weather had been so nice in Anchorage. We were on a greater adventure than we had anticipated. Generally, the road was easier to drive than it had been in the summertime. There were no pot holes and no frost heaves to contend with. The snow plow makes all things even and smooth!

We continued on and drove to California with no problems. I don't know if I will ever drive the Alaska Highway in the winter time again, but I wouldn't take anything for the experience. I know it can be done and I'm glad that we were blessed with the opportunity to do it. It's one of those things that you do that

ives you a feeling of accomplishment, even if thousands of
thers have done the same thing before you.

Our motor home on the Alaska Highway.

Hitched up and headed south on the Alaska Highway.

Chapter 26: The Wreck

We left the Holiday Mountain RV Park in Mountain View, Arkansas and headed south, toward Memphis, Tennessee. We drove about one hundred and thirty miles and pulled onto I-40, headed east. It was a beautiful, sunny day. The winds were calm and the traffic was not heavy. I intended to go to the Hermitage Landing RV Park in Nashville and spend a night or two there.

I had the cruise control set on about sixty MPH and the highway was in good shape and we were making good time approaching the Tennessee border. We were still in Arkansas about twenty miles out of Memphis, Tennessee. I had come up behind an eighteen wheeler trailer truck. The red truck, which showed a lot of age, was pulling an empty flat bed trailer probably forty feet long. He was doing about fifty eight MPH and so I put my blinker on, checked my mirrors and pulled out into the passing lane. I was slowly passing him up, still running with the cruise control on. The headlights on my Suburban were just even with the driver's door on the truck as we approached the on ramp coming off highway 149 onto I-40. The on ramp is very short and the 'third' lane doesn't run very far before it runs out.

A large truck, pulling two large trailers, was coming onto I-40. All three of us arrived at the end of the third lane at the same time. The truck with the two trailers pulled abruptly over into the outside lane. *(I guess it was just too much trouble for him to put his foot on his brakes and slow down until we had passed.)*

The driver of the old, red truck with the empty flat bed trailer, pulled over into my lane! I pulled over as far to my left as could, to keep him from hitting me. I got on the brakes, which disengaged the cruise control, and I saw the old, red truck start to pull ahead of me.

In the next second, our trailer was right beside the driver's door! That's what it looked like to me, any way. Then the trailer whipped around and came up on my wife's side of the Suburban! Then it was back on my side!

I reached down in an attempt to find the little handle that was mounted under the steering wheel column that activated the trailer brakes. The truck was being so violently shaken and being pushed from one lane of traffic to the other, that I couldn't find it! I had to hold the steering wheel as tightly as I could, just to try to keep the Suburban and trailer on the highway.

There we were coming down I-40 using both lanes and both shoulders of the road. My wife and I are Christians and we read the Bible every day. The Bible tells us that there is power in the name of Jesus and I'll tell you right now that we were both calling on JESUS!!! The trailer was still coming up on my side of the Suburban and then coming around and up on my wife' side. We must have gone down the highway like that for at least half a mile.

Finally the truck started to spin around backwards. The trailer was still flopping around all over the highway. It seemed that things were happening in slow motion. The truck turned hard to the right and we started hearing a lot of crunching and scratching and tearing sounds. Finally, our rig scraped and rattled to a stop! We were still alive! The two eighteen wheelers had sped away.

I asked my wife if she was hurt and she said no. I told her to get out and get off to the side of the highway, fearing that someone behind us might run into us. She jumped out of the truck and hopped off into the grass on the side of the shoulder of the road.

I got out on my side and ran over to her. I looked back down the interstate toward the direction we had come from. There was traffic in both lanes backed up for about a mile. They could all see what was happening and had backed off and given us plenty of room.

The trailer had come to a stop on the shoulder of the road and looked as if I had just pulled over and parked it. The truck was still hooked up to the trailer hitch, but it was turned around and facing the trailer! The entire right front corner of the trailer was split open and buckled up. The propane gas bottles had come off the rack and were lying on the road in front of the trailer. The sway bar had snapped off and had dug up a portion of the asphalt road.

The rear quarter panel window on the Suburban was shattered from it's collision with the corner of the travel trailer,

ut the glass was still in place. The rear fender was also
dented up.

I walked over to the drivers side of the trailer and could see
no visible damage, other than the tires were shredded and the
rims were all eaten up where they had scraped, sometimes
sideways, along the highway. There were skid marks headed off
down the highway as far as I could see. I checked again to make
sure my wife was all right and we thanked the Lord for keeping
us from getting hurt. The way we figured it, although our "stuff"
was damaged, we could always get more "stuff," but there was
only one of each of us.

When I had pulled over to my left to avoid hitting the truck,
or to avoid him hitting me, I had evidently run off the paved
portion of the road with the left side of the trailer and truck,
although I really don't remember running off the road. The two
tires on the driver's side of the trailer were blown out and the
left rear tire on the Suburban was blown out too!

In a matter of seconds people started pulling over to make
sure we were OK and to offer their assistance. A considerate
man and his wife, who told me that they were on their way to
Memphis for a concert, stopped and let me use their cell phone
to call the police and to call my towing service. We didn't have a
cell phone at this time. I must have stayed on his cell phone for
thirty minutes or more and he refused to let me compensate him
for the charges. There are some really nice people in this world!
I don't know his name, but thanks again and more thanks!

After I knew that the police and the wrecker truck were on the way, I walked back to the trailer and opened the door. We were not prepared for what we were about to see. Every cabinet and drawer had been forced open by the violence of the trailer whipping back and forth and everything, and I mean **EVERYTHING**, was in the middle of the floor! Everything had flown out of the refrigerator and was lying, broken in the kitchen part of the trailer. The microwave was hanging by its electric cord and dangling in space. Books, video tapes, broken dishes, magazines, food, canned goods, clothing, medicines,

A strange and unpleasant smell also greeted us as we went inside. Vinegar, cooking oil, hot sauce, everything that was packaged in glass containers was broken on the floor. Someone had given us a gift set of four jars of jelly. The jars were broken and the jelly was every where. It did add a touch of color to the mess.

Standing inside the front bedroom, you could look outside...*through the wall!*

I spied out my camera bag and everything seemed to be alright so I took our video camera and our 35mm camera and took pictures of our wreck so we could show the folks back home what had happened to us. *(Tour guides to the end!)*

Soon the State Trooper arrived and filled out the accident report. He told me that just a few days before there was another RV wrecked on this section of the interstate, but the people had been killed. He told us that we were lucky, but we knew that Jesus had taken care of us and that luck didn't have a thing to do with it! He didn't give me a traffic ticket, although here I was, sitting on the side of the road with a wrecked truck and trailer and no one in sight that had anything to do with the accident, but me. I described the trucks to him, but I hadn't gotten any license information and I knew the information would be useless.

The wrecker truck got there and the Trooper left. After surveying the damage, the wrecker truck driver told me he had to go to town to get another wrecker truck, because he couldn't pull the Suburban and the trailer at the same time with the truck he had brought with him.

I told him that I didn't know if my Suburban had to be towed, since I had shut the engine off myself and I couldn't see any damage, except to the rear quarter panel, the window and the tire. We both looked under the truck and there was nothing leaking and no apparent damage. He decided to try to turn the Suburban around facing the way it was supposed to face and see if it was OK. He hooked the cable from the wrecker truck under the truck frame and I got in and started the engine and put the transmission in neutral, so we wouldn't hurt it and he pulled the truck around. I tried to help by turning the front wheels. The truck came around easily. It was still hooked up to the trailer hitch.

We couldn't see any damage to the frame of the trailer or the trailer axles. I couldn't see why I just couldn't pull the trailer off with my Suburban and neither could the wrecker truck driver. He took the blown out tire off the Suburban and replaced it with the spare. I had only one spare tire for the trailer, so the wrecker truck driver headed back to town to get me another tire and rim.

While he was gone, I put the gas bottles in the back end of the Suburban. They were not ruptured and the rubber hoses that connected them to the trailer were not damaged.
I got out my trusty duct tape and covered the shattered Suburban window inside and out, to keep the glass from falling out as I drove down the highway.

Meanwhile, my wife was in the trailer, trying to sort things out and put things back where they came from. She had a **BIG** job! I put the microwave back up in the cabinet and then went back outside and got my tool box out of the back of the Suburban. I took some dry wall screws and started screwing the metal siding into the wooden frame of the travel trailer. After lovingly 'tapping' the aluminum siding back into place, as close to it's original place as I could get it, I screwed it down with the dry wall screws.

Pretty soon the wrecker truck was back with a new tire and rim and he changed out the two blown out tires on the trailer. I paid him for the tire and rim and he left. My wife had just about picked up everything and was mopping the floor.

We got into the truck and continued heading east. We had been on the side of I-40 for about five hours.

We drove another hundred miles and stopped in Jackson, Tennessee. We were still shook up from our ordeal and I'll tell you I kept a close eye on that trailer as we pulled it down the road! Once set up in the campground we continued to clean and set things back into some kind of order. I went outside and put more dry wall screws into the aluminum siding. Back inside, I used more dry wall screws to put the paneling back up. It was broken and split and had fallen off the wall. We stopped and bought more duct tape to add to the shattered rear window of "Herbie," the nick name we called our Suburban.

Tip: It is always a good idea to have some good towing and road service insurance. If I had not had this insurance it would have cost me hundreds of dollars in fees instead of just paying for the tire and rim.

I called the insurance company the next day. They advised me to go to the Coachmen dealer in Nashville and arrangements would be made for an adjuster to come over and estimate the damages. I called the dealer when I arrived in Nashville and after telling him what the problem was, he advised me to go to the Coachmen travel trailer factory in Fitzgerald, Georgia. He explained to me that if I allowed the repairs to be made at the dealership, that it would just take more time, because the parts had to be ordered, made and shipped from the factory any way.

I would save a lot of time if I could go directly to the factory. He also told me that the factory was equipped with a repair facility that could handle the repair of my trailer better and a lot faster than he could.

The man at the dealership gave me the factory telephone number and after a call we were headed south on I-75 to Fitzgerald.

We arrived at the Coachmen factory and I was told to unhook the trailer in the parking lot. A man driving a tractor came over and took our trailer and backed it into a slot right behind the office building. The trailer was plugged into a thirty amp electric outlet and hooked up to water. We were told that we could stay in our trailer until the repairs began. I was on the telephone several times with the insurance company. The adjuster showed up six days later.

After the factory made a repair estimate and the insurance adjuster made a repair estimate, *(the insurance companies estimate was higher!)* our repairs began.

The trailer was towed to the repair building and they started to dismantle the broken parts. They were going to have to replace the front of the trailer and the right side of the trailer, from the door forward. I would also have to have a new trailer hitch. When the sway bar had snapped off, it had damaged the unit. All of the counter tops in the kitchen and in the bathroom would have to be replaced. The kitchen table was going to have o be replaced also. When everything had been thrown out of all the cabinets, what ever hit the counter tops and table had chipped and cracked the Formica.

We moved into a brand new motel. After a couple of nights at the motel, I went back to the factory to check on things and I was talking to the plant manger. He asked me how I liked that new motel. I told him that we didn't like it at all. I told him that we were campers and we liked to stay in our camper. We knew who slept in our bed and who used our bathroom and who brushed their teeth in the lavatory, all assurances that we didn't have at the motel, even if it was brand new. He told me not to leave without seeing him and I went back to the repair facility to see how the work was progressing. I stopped by his office on the way out. The plant manager was outside and a man was backing a big thirty-four foot motor home into the parking space behind the office. The driver got out of the motor home, walked over and handed the keys to the motor home to the plant manger, and he turned and handed them to me. He told me that we could stay in the motor home until our trailer was finished being repaired!

Wait! It gets better! The factory reimbursed me for the two night motel bill!

While waiting for the trailer we put our time to good use. We had the window repaired on the Suburban and also had the windshield replaced while we were at it, since it had a good crack in it from a rock thrown from the real wheel of a gravel truck.

While we waited on repairs we attended the "Wild Hog Festival" in Abbeville, Georgia....no kidding! We drove over and saw where Jefferson Davis was captured after the Civil War.

Finally the day to get our travel trailer back had arrived. It was May 18th. We had wrecked it on April 27th.

While the trailer was in the repair facility I had them install new stabilizing jacks. They resealed all the windows, made us a new TV shelf and fixed a bad spot in the floor right in front of the door for no charge. We were treated to a factory tour by the plant manager and generally treated like royalty the entire time we were there.

The trailer was finally brought up to the front and I was hooking it up to the Suburban when the plant manager came over and asked me what I was doing? I told him I was hooking up and planned to drive up to Unadilla. Georgia. He wouldn't let us go! The factory was having a fish fry for the employees that night and he insisted that we stay and eat fried fish! No arm twisting needed on Cajuns when it comes to eating fish, so we gladly stayed!

The next day we were back on the road. The trailer looked better than it did before it had been damaged, inside and out. I was still a little nervous as I pulled the trailer up I-75. The trailer didn't feel like it was pulling right and after several times when the trailer seemed to be driving the truck, I had the adjustable trailer hitch readjusted. I had this done two or three times and the trailer never did pull right, *(as far as I was concerned, any way.)* I guess some of it was just 'shell shock' from the accident, but I never did trust that trailer to follow along behind me like it was supposed to do after that.

Almost six months later a mechanic at Camping World in Nashville finally adjusted the trailer hitch to the position it was supposed to be in and the trailer towed a lot better, but I never again felt at ease while I towed it around at highway speed…and most of the time I towed it at less than the speed limit. We were "on the road again," as the song goes. The adventure continued…..but at a little slower pace while we were towing the trailer!

Looks like I need a longer trailer hitch!

Testing the frame on our Coachmen trailer.

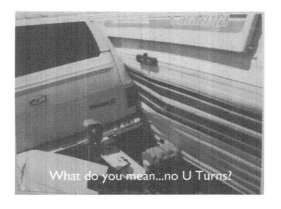

What do you mean...no U Turns?

Chapter 27: Trying To See It All

We pulled into Unadilla, Georgia and stopped at Southern Trails Resort. The resort is built in a large pecan grove. If you happen to be there in the fall, you can have your own private pecan harvest!

We washed and waxed our trailer and our Suburban. Most campgrounds will not allow you wash your rig, but we were allowed to here. If you like to play Bingo, then Southern Trails is the place for you, with several Bingo nights each week.

We drove up to Tennessee on I-75. Every now and then one of those big trailer trucks would 'sneak' up on me and when the wind he was pushing would hit our trailer, it felt to me, like the trailer was going out of control again. I must have a strong heart, because I didn't have heart failure every time this happened. I was still nervous from the wreck.

I took a lot of video pictures wherever we went. I had an 8mm Sony and was taking pictures of everything that moved and everything that didn't move. It was great...you didn't have to get the film developed! You could take all the pictures you wanted and then see them on TV as soon as you got home. And there was sound too! I learned to talk to my camera, so I could tell everyone what they were seeing when they watched the tape. Later I purchased a small editor so I could add some music to the background. I had become a producer, director and camera man, as well as actor, announcer, editor and distributor.

I would shoot loads of video tape and then bring it back to the camper, where I would edit the tape down *(too much video of the same thing is boring and I always had too much video of the same thing)* and put some music on it and send copies to our family and friends. They got to see what we were seeing and I sure would rather send a video *(it was fun to work on)* rather than write letters. We heard some good comments on our Video Letters. Of course we did send videos to some folks who have never acknowledged, to this day, that they ever looked at them or had any intention to do so.

I pulled into a mall at Pigeon Forge, Tennessee so my wife could get some exercise.....you know, exercise her ability to find all the bargains in the mall. I got out and felt the wheel hubs on the trailer. The two rear wheel hubs were very hot. The wheel bearings needed to be changed. I didn't know if this was a result of the accident or what, but when the wheel bearings are hot that means that they aren't working properly. If left to themselves, they will eventually come apart and you may see one of the trailer wheels and tires passing you up as you are driving down the road.

I *"forced"* my wife to go shopping in the mall. I jacked the trailer up and pulled one of the wheels off, took off the brake hub and removed the bearings from the axle. It is really not that ard of a job, but it is messy and greasy. I had repacked the wheel bearings, on other trailers as well as this one, in the past.

I caught the trolley and told the driver that I needed an auto parts store. I brought the bearings that I had taken off the axle to match up the parts, bought a couple of sets of bearings and returned to the mall parking lot, where I changed the bearings in both wheels on the rear axle of the trailer.

Although I was out in the parking lot with axle grease up to my elbows, several men stopped and actually asked if I needed help. That's Southern Hospitality at its finest!

Really! I love to grease bearings.

Greasing Wheel Bearings in Branson, Mo.

We visited the mountains in Tennessee and North Carolina and were off through Virginia and stopped to visit Washington D.C. again. We had been there before, but the new Holocaust Museum had just opened and we wanted to tour it. Talk about *DEPRESSING!* It is, but if in Washington, D.C. don't miss it! I don't know if I can say that it was a 'joy' to tour this museum, but it's something everyone should see. We walked through one of the actual boxcars that the Nazi Germans used to haul all of those people off to the gas chambers in. It sure made the hairs on the back of my neck stand up! The room full of empty shoes that were taken from the victims touched us deeply. Many tourists have shed tears in this place.

We towed up to Pennsylvania and toured Gettysburg and some of the Amish communities with names like 'Intercourse' and 'Bird in Hand.' Those Amish people sure know how to cook!

We drove onward through Pennsylvania and into New Jersey. We made reservations at Liberty Harbor RV Park in Jersey City. We got off the interstate and down into the city following the directions to the park. It looked like something we saw in a movie. The buildings were painted in graffiti and some of them looked like they had been bombed out and abandoned for years. We felt better when we arrived at the campground, because there was a security guard at the gate and he had a gun....then we saw the view. Sitting outside the door of the trailer you could see the Statue of Liberty and Ellis Island. We were directly across from the World Trade Center *(this was before 9/11)* and off in the distance was the Empire State Building! At night the entire city of New York was ablaze in lights….and it was all just for us!

We took the subway over into New York City for the first two days of site seeing, but after some kind soul explained to my wife that the subway ran **under** the river, we took the Hoboken Ferry over after that.

We did all the New York things, and another of my child hood dreams came true. I went all the way to the top of the Empire State Building! It was great! It could only have been better if King Kong was still climbing up and I'd have gotten to see him. *(Of course we did see him in Florida and in California at Universal Studios.)*

I went up to the top of the World Trade Center. *(This was before the sad day of 9/11)* I know it's higher than the Empire State Building, but it just wasn't as exciting to me. As a child, my dream was of seeing the Empire State building one day. I checked off another dream come true and we continued on seeing the sites.

I ate the best Italian Sausage in a deli down on the Battery and I still dream about that sausage sometimes even now.

The people in New York City treated us great. We had heard all the stories of how people wouldn't talk to you and how rude everyone was, but they talked to us! Every one treated us very courteously and the people were friendly and helpful. We enjoyed the city and we were not robbed or murdered at all!

We headed up to New England and had fun in Plymouth and Boston, Massachusetts. My mother flew up and joined us. My sister and her husband were living near Boston at the time and we had a mini family reunion. We cooked up a bunch of lobsters, Cajun style. They tasted wonderful. I wish I had some more of them to eat right now!

While in Massachusetts we took the ferry out to Nantucket and then over to Martha's Vineyard. We spent a lot of time on boats that day. We took a bus tour of Nantucket that sticks in my mind. The bus driver raced down the road about two hundred miles and hour shouting what we were supposed to be seeing out of the windows. He would announce what was to be seen up ahead and I would point my camera out the window, but by the time I had the camera ready, the point of interest had disappeared and was about three miles back! If I was not a Christian man, I would have severely injured that driver! If I ever go back I'm going to rent one of those little motor bikes and take a lot more time to really see the island.

We went on up into Maine and spent some time exploring the coast at Moody Beach.

We took our rig up to Bar Harbor and drove the Suburban up on Cadillac Mountain, where you can be the first person in the US to see the sun rise. We weren't the first to see it, because the sun just came up too early while we were there.

We stopped in Lubec, Maine and drove across the Canadian border onto Campobello Island where President Franklin Roosevelt had a 'cottage.' It was here where he was stricken with polio. There are several light houses to be seen 'close up' in this area and if you are a lighthouse enthusiast, this is the place for you.

We drove over into Canada into New Brunswick for a stop in St. John. We saw the Reversing Falls. The tidal range is so great here that at low tide the St. John River flows out into the Bay of Fundy, but at high tide (the tides can range forty or fifty feet in the Bay of Fundy) the river reverses it's direction and runs back inland.

At Fundy Bay National Park we saw boats tied to the dock, but sitting on the dry ocean bottom and then when the tide came in, only hours later, these same boats were riding high in the water even with the top of the dock.

After visiting the Anne Murray Museum in Spring Hill, we traveled on into Nova Scotia and into the town of Baddeck

In Baddeck we had a chance to go on board the "Blue Nose II,' a replica of the famous sailing boat that is pictured on all the

Canadian dimes. Now when we are in the Circle Vision Theater, in O' Canada, at EPCOT center at Disney World and they show the Blue Nose up on that giant screen, we just stand there and think, "Oh, yes, we've been aboard."

We drove the Coast Trail on Cape Breton Island and walked the streets of the Fortress of Louisbourg, which totally fascinated me. We saw the archeological dig on Grassy Island, went to Sherbrook Village, rode the Halifax-Dartmouth ferry, wandered all over the Citadel, went to the Maritime Museum and saw artifacts from the Titanic and even drove over to the cemetery and visited the graves of some of the Titanic's victims.

We ate at Wendy's in Halifax and discovered that they had the ninety-nine cent menu. With the exchange rate at that time, we were eating those ninety-nine cent hamburgers for sixty-five cents American!

We drove out to Peggy's Cove and saw the beautiful lighthouse. The lighthouse is a post office now. This is one of the most photographed places in Nova Scotia.

We saw Fort Anne at Annapolis Royal, walked through the Victoria Gardens, attended the annual festival at Windsor, and visited the place where they kicked some of my Cajun ancestors out of Nova Scotia at Grand Pre.

We took the ferry over to Prince Edward Island and saw Green Gables, where Anne lived. There were waves twelve to fifteen feet high in Northumberland Strait, which greatly thrilled my wife. The ferry is free to cross over onto Prince Edward Island, but you have to pay to get back. I understand that you can drive across the new bridge now, so you no longer have to take the ferry.

We saw everything we could see and then headed back south. We visited family back in Louisiana and then went out to California and then to Oregon where we visited our sons and then decided to go back to Alaska, where we stayed for almost two years.

We traded off our trailer in Anchorage and drove the Alaska Highway in the winter and picked up our new thirty-four foot Bounder motor home in California.

We have traveled up and down and across our great country. We have been to the top of the Empire State Building in New York City, saw the Hollywood sign in Los Angeles, watched the Space Shuttle launch four times. *(Two day launches and two night launches.)*

We ate real Mexican food....in Mexico, white water rafted in Tennessee and then in Alaska. We have looked down into the Grand Canyon and landed in an airplane on skies on Denali *(Mt. McKinley.)* We have seen Key West and roamed around Nova Scotia and all the other provinces of Canada. We have been out to Alcatraz in San Francisco Bay, panned for gold in the Yukon and caught Halibut in the Cook Inlet. We saw all the lights on the "strip" in Las Vegas, saw the Northern Lights, and wandered around in the desert in Arizona.

We saw all the Presidents carved into the mountain in South Dakota and drank 5 cent coffee at Wall Drugs. We took the ferry to Victoria British Columbia, drove all over Death Valley, saw the Hoover Dam, been to the Petrified Forrest, saw dinosaur tracks in Glen Rose, Texas and traveled down Highway 1 from Oregon to Los Angles.

Have we seen it all? *NO!* I don't know if anyone can see it all, but give us credit, we are trying!

June & the McClellands at Disney World

Lyle Chauvin and I with two Kenai River Kings

Doing time on the Rock...Alcatraz.

What time do they eat around here?

Its in Arizona....not London!

Me, June, Randy Jr. and Emmitt on a California beach.

June at Green Gables in Prince Edward Island, Canada.

Boot Hill in Tombstone, Arizona.

Randy Jr. and June overlooking San Francisco.

How do we get to the other side?

GRAND CANYON NATIONAL PARK

Guess where we are?

Chapter 28: Fire!

We took possession of our new Bounder and after several days of unloading the Suburban and trying to find a place to put everything we were on the road again. It was up to Las Vegas, where we bought a new Saturn car. Now we had three things that were new to us, a motor home, a car and *monthly bills!*

We went down to Laughlin, Nevada and then up through Kingman, Arizona to Williams, where we took a side trip to the Grand Canyon National Park. I still can't get over how those people let their kids stand up on those narrow, rock walls so they could take pictures of them. One slip and it's a mile straight down before you hit the bottom of the canyon.

We pulled into Flagstaff and paid for one nights rent at Greer's Pine Shadows RV Park. I plugged in the electric, hooked up the water hose and strung out the sewer hose and then we jumped into the car and took off to see Sedona, a beautiful town about twenty-five miles south of Flagstaff. We drove around and took some video pictures and then headed back to the RV Park.

We were almost to Flagstaff when we noticed a large forest fire up on the side of a mountain. I told my wife to get the video camera and take some pictures for our next video letter. As we drove on toward the campground, we got closer and closer to the fire. We took some more pictures. As we got closer to the RV Park the traffic got heavier and people started driving like they were crazy, like they were in a really big hurry. The traffic became heavier and heavier, came to a slow crawl and finally all but stopped.

I could see a police officer in the middle of the road and he wasn't letting any traffic proceed straight ahead on the road that we needed to take to go to our motor home. I got out the road map and could see a couple of side roads that 'might' get me closer to the campground and I decided to chance it. It was a sure thing that the policeman wasn't going to let us get through. I turned off and started following the road map and came out about a quarter of a mile south of the RV Park.

When we couldn't get any closer I parked the car, and we walked up to the RV park. When we got there, fire hoses were running up the entrance road and into the campground. The employees of the park met us at the gate. We were advised that the Fire Marshall had given orders to evacuate the park. I told the park attendant that I wanted to get my motor home out of the park, but he wouldn't let us in. We could see some fire trucks and other equipment at the back of the campground and the whole mountain behind the park was covered with dense, white smoke.

There were several airplanes flying overhead, dumping water and red, fire retardant on the side of the mountain. I was worried about my motor home being damaged or burned, but I have to admit that it was pretty exciting too. I had never been around a large a forest fire before and this one seemed to be pretty big.

We stood outside of the gate for about an hour. We didn't have any place else to go and at least we knew the motor home was OK for the time being. We could see it parked not far into the campground close to the front gate.

One of the park workers came outside the gate and advised us that we were going to have to leave, because the planes were going to dump some fire retardant on the campground! I told him that I had all the roof vents open and I asked permission to at least go and close them. He told me NO! He told me that no one was allowed into the RV Park by order of the Fire Marshall. Then he told us that we had to leave...NOW!

We walked back up to the car and just hung around. There were other people in the parking lot that had been barred from the resort also. The concern was on all of our faces and the consensus was that we should have been allowed to remove our rigs and all of our belongings from the resort.

Every few minutes a low flying plane would dump water or retardant on the side of the mountain. I was trying to judge if the retardant had fallen in the campground or just close to it, but there was no way to tell for sure.

We stayed in the parking lot with the car for about another hour and a half. Finally I decided that I just had to walk back up the road and check on my new Bounder. We had only had the new motor home for about three weeks, and now it was held captive by strangers in a campground we had never even seen before.

I walked back up the street with my wife and another man whose rig was in the park also. As we approached the entrance gate, I saw a Fire Department tank truck come out of the campground. There was a large fire hose that went all the way across the four lane street and up into the driveway and then to the back of the RV park where the other fire trucks were still parked with their red lights flashing. The truck came out of the park and drove across the street following the hose and went into the parking lot of the strip mall across the street. Then he was able to drive around the hose and back onto the street.

There was a fireman standing in the middle of the street. I guess he was there to make sure no one came along and ran over the hose. There was no traffic and he was just standing here looking in the direction of the fire equipment at the rear of the park.

I walked up to him and said, "Sir, I need to get that motor home over there out of the park." I pointed over to our Bounder which was plainly visible from the street. I asked, "Can I follow along the hose here and get back onto the street like that tank truck did?"

"Sure. That'll be OK, but hurry up," he said.

I turned to my wife and told her to go back to the car and watch for me and to follow me when I passed, because I didn't know where I was going to go with the motor home once it was rescued from its RV park bondage.

There was no one at the entrance to the campground when I walked through the gate and I quickly walked over to my Bounder. I opened the side compartment and disconnected the electric plug and threw the wire in. I hurriedly shut the water off and disconnected the hose and threw it into the compartment with the electric plug. I was putting the sewer hose up into another compartment, when one of the campground employees suddenly appeared, standing behind me.

"You are not supposed to be in the park!" he told me. I explained to him that I had permission from the fireman to get my motor home out of the park. By this time I had shut all the compartments and was walking around the motor home to get in the door. The man told me, "I can't let you move that motor home out of here!"

"Don't get in front of me," I told him as calmly as I could muster. "I'm getting out of here while I have the chance and the permission of the Fire Department."

I got in and started the engine and pulled out of the driveway and into the street. I don't know where the campground guy disappeared to. You know...you just can't give some people any authority. Their head starts to swell and they become dictators!

My wife had prepared the electric coffee pot before we left to go to Sedona and I didn't notice it sitting there on the kitchen cabinet. It was full of water and had some good Louisiana Community coffee and chicory already measured out and sitting in the coffee filter in the metal basket of the pot. When I went down the driveway and onto the road, I had to make a pretty sharp left turn. The coffee pot slid off the cabinet and I heard a loud thud. I looked back and saw the water from the coffee pot running across the floor. There was not much that I could do about it, so I continued on.

I went around the hose and back onto the street and headed toward I-40. My wife saw me coming and fell in right behind me. We pulled into a gas station a few miles down the street. We cleaned up the coffee pot mess, gassed up the motor home and the car, hooked the car up to the tow bar and headed east on the interstate highway.

I drove about forty or fifty miles and stopped at the Meteor Crater RV Park. I asked the attendant if there were any shade trees in the campground. He told me that there were no trees in the park at all, so I told him, "Good! I'll stay the night!"

A few days later my wife wrote a letter to Greer's Pine Shadows RV Park asking them to refund our camping fee. We had not spent but about fifteen minutes in our rig while it was parked at the resort and we felt that we had been treated badly during the forest fire by their employees. The only thing we used had been the water to fill up our coffee pot. We mailed the letter and after eight years we are still waiting for their response.

Four day later we were staying at the Red Arrow RV Park in Edgewood, New Mexico. I was sitting at the dinette eating lunch. I heard my wife say, "Oh No! Not again!"

I looked out the window and could see flames about fifty feet high! I jumped up and went to the door. **The prairie was on fire!**

I walked toward the fire and I could see a lot of other people coming out of their rigs and headed toward the direction of the fire also. The fire was across the interstate highway from us. I walked back to the RV and retrieved the video camera. I went back to where the other people were watching the fire. I was amazed at how quickly the fire spread. The fire was traveling parallel with the interstate just across from us and I know in my heart that I took much better video than the TV stations did.

There were some horses in a fenced in field and they didn't like the idea of that fire at all. They couldn't get out of the field, but they ran around and around and around that field as fast as they could. I guess they thought they were getting away. The fire came close to them, but they escaped unharmed in the end.

The fire roared on for about an hour before it was brought under control. It didn't come near the RV Park, but we sure kept an eye out in case of another blaze. I even filled up the fresh water tank and put up the hoses, rolled up the awnings, etc, just in case we had to leave in a hurry!

Chapter 29: Tornado!

We went back to Louisiana to visit family and friends and to show off our new Bounder motor home. We decided to drive over to Mississippi and spend some time on the Mississippi Gulf Coast. We were camped at the Mississippi Pines Resort in Picayune. It had been raining for about a week and the weather was dreary that day also.

I had a defective mattress in the motor home and the dealership in Picayune had ordered a new one for us and I was waiting for it to come in. The mattress had not come in, so I went up to the office to pay for another night.

I walked into the office and saw that the man behind the desk was giving some directions to a lady. The office at Mississippi Pines is a log cabin with a nice front porch and there were two big, wooden rocking chairs on the porch. It was drizzling rain and it was getting darker by the minute although it was early afternoon.

I stepped back out of the office, onto the front porch, waiting to talk to the man behind the desk. All of a sudden the two rocking chairs flew off up into the air and landed across the street!

I looked up and the trees in the park were being twisted and pushed by an extremely brutal wind that had come down, out of the sky. I could see the pattern of the wind in the tall pines...it was circular and of great force. The log building was shuddering and trembling. It was a tornado and I was in the center of it!

Trees started snapping and breaking limbs were flying everywhere. There was a large sign in the middle of the road and it blew over and landed about fifty yards away.

I stood there and looked up into the center of the tornado! I know that they have made some movies lately and in all the movies someone usually looks up into the center of the thing and that brings the movie to a great climax, but this was no movie. This was really happening and it was happening to me!

My wife was in the motor home and this tornado was headed straight for her!

I screamed at the top of my voice, "In the name of Jesus, you go back up in the sky where you belong! I bind you up tornado! In the name of Jesus you are not going to hurt my wife or anything we own!"

The two people in the office heard me….I was yelling louder than the tornado…they couldn't help but hear me. They had a look of total fear on their faces. I didn't know if they were afraid of the storm, or because of me standing in the doorway of the porch screaming at a tornado in the Name of Jesus! *(If this sounds crazy to you, it's all in the Bible.)*

The tornado was headed straight for our motor home, which was parked about two blocks from where I was standing.

My wife was cooking in the kitchen, when she heard what sounded like a freight train coming fast. She realized that it was a tornado and that she should do something and was pondering whether she should go outside or lay on the floor. She had never been in a tornado before and all the things that she had heard over the years, the things that you are supposed to do and not supposed to do came flooding through her mind.

The motor home was hit with violent wind and my wife thought that it was going to turn over on its side. Then the motor home settled back down and the wind pushed it so that he thought it was going to turn over on the other side! All she had time to do was crouch down on the floor and call upon the Name of Jesus too!

There was some kind of an electric meter and box that was on a metal pole across the street from the front of the motor home. The pole was cemented about three feet into the ground. The force of the tornado sucked that pole out of the ground and sent it all up. Immediately our electric serviced was gone!

The force of the wind tore awnings off trailers and motor homes and deposited them in other camping sites. There was a small motor home parked across the street from the office and a large tree limb cut a gash about three feet long in the side of the unit.

There was several wire baskets positioned around the park where aluminum cans were collected for recycling. The tornado sucked up all the cans out of the wire baskets and spread them out for about a hundred yards. The baskets however remained in place.

Along with the tornado came a torrential down pour. I was still standing on the porch and all I could think about was my wife. I ran out and got into my car to go back to the motor home. The street that I would have normally driven down was blocked by a large tree that had fallen across the road. I had to drive completely around the campground to find a clear road headed back toward our RV.

I pulled up in the front of the motor home and I could see my wife through the windshield. I was greatly relieved that she was OK. The space where I normally parked the car was occupied by a large branch that had been torn out of a nearby tree. If would have been 'home' that branch would have fallen on the car and caused untold damage!

The tornado had come through the side of the RV Park where we were parked. On the other end of the park, not so much as a leaf had blown over!

Tree limbs and even some whole trees, had been blown down and some cars and RVs were damaged. No one was injured that I know of and the damage was minimal. Of course, I guess the people who had their awnings ripped off thought the damage was a little more than minimal.

My awning was rolled up. I never leave my awning extended when there is any chance of bad weather. On several occasions I have seen awnings blown over and damaged by a passing thunder storm.

The tornado had headed straight for our motor home from the resort office. When the storm ripped the electric pole out of the ground across the street from the RV, it made a sharp right turn and went back up into the sky! *(I tell you that there IS power in the Name of Jesus!)* It broke the tops off a bunch of trees across the street from the park, but way up, about thirty or forty feet off the ground.

I couldn't find any damage to the motor home right after the tornado had passed, but later when I went to clean the windshield, I found lots of tiny peck marks in the glass and two 'bulls eye' chips. The wind in the storm had picked up some of the gravel from off the streets and thrown it into our windshield! Our car was not damaged.

I have had people tell me they don't want to go up to Alaska for fear that their windshields would be cracked or broken, and here we were sitting perfectly still in a RV park...and had been sitting there for seven days, without moving an inch...and now our windshield was damaged! But we were not hurt! We were in good shape and now we just use those peck marks in the windshield to show people where the tornado hit us.

They couldn't get our electric going right away so I had to move the motor home to another site. I pulled over to the side of the park that the tornado missed!

Five days later we were camped at Leesburg RV Resort in Leesburg, Alabama. We had driven up to meet my brother and his wife to do a little camping together. We drank a lot of coffee and sat in our lawn chairs by the lake and watched my little, nephew fish in the lake.

That night the forecast was for extremely bad weather. I went into the motor home and tuned in to the Weather Channel. *(I call it the bad weather channel.)* They were predicting extremely severe thunderstorms for our area and had issued a tornado warning.

We sat outside and watched the weather. I was not overjoyed by the forecast, after what had just happened to us in Mississippi. The clouds were building up and the lightning could be seen flashing in the distance.

My brother and his family went back to their travel trailer, which was parked across the campground and June and I retired into our motor home.

It wasn't very long before the rain started. It wasn't just a regular rain, it was a deluge. It rained and rained and the wind gusted enough to shake the motor home. I tuned into the local TV station *(small satellite dishes don't do very well in extremely heavy rain)* and they were having continuous weather reporting.

The National Weather Center had issued a special Tornado Warning and the announcer kept telling us over and over that this kind of special warning was only issued once or twice a year. This boosted our moral greatly!

The lightning became more and more severe and rain was still coming down by the buckets full. Then the weather man came on the TV and said, "There has been a tornado sited on the ground three miles west of Leesburg and the tornado is headed east. We were just south of the city limits of Leesburg! The tornado was coming in our direction! We were glued to the TV set. That weather man sure had our undivided attention. Then in the next second there appeared on the TV screen a guy and gal trying to sell us a new Ford pick up truck!

I couldn't believe it. A tornado was headed our way, but that wasn't as important as a commercial!

I hurriedly changed the TV channel…no other station was evidently aware of the weather situation. They had on regular programming.

I flipped the TV back to the channel that had the weather reports. The weather man came back on after the commercials and went on reporting and reporting and not one time did he ever bring up the subject of that tornado that was supposed to be on the ground and headed our way again!

We stayed up until about four AM, until the weather system had passed on through and then we went to bed. My brother, Mike, had stayed up all night also, but his wife, Suzanne, had had a pleasant nights sleep. It's a good thing that all of us were up guarding her all night, making sure she was safe!

We were parked on the lake shore and by the next afternoon the water had risen so much in the lake that we had to move our rig to higher ground. Other than that we were OK. Just another chapter in our book of adventures!

Chapter 30: Post Script

We were coming down Highway 1 in southern British Columbia, headed south. It had been raining all day and was getting late in the afternoon. We were approaching the Hell's Gate tourist attraction and were discussing if we should stop there.

We could see a lot of small rocks rolling down the mountain side that went straight up from the highway on the drivers side of the Suburban. (We were pulling our Coachmen trailer.) I looked up and saw a very **LARGE** rock rolling down the mountain at us.

I hit the brake and kept looking at that rock. It was getting closer and closer. I tried to do some mental math to plot the course of the rock to see if I should speed up or slow down. I opted for slow and stop if I could get it! I locked up the brakes as the rock rolled onto the highway and then...I ran over it with a loud bang and a loud thud!

We were at the entrance to the Hell's Gate parking lot, so I slowly pulled in and stopped the rig. I could hear the rock dragging under the rig. I got out and looked under the truck. I saw nothing and so I went back and kneeled down on the wet pavement and looked under the trailer. I saw the rock. It was lying up against the front axle of the trailer. I had to get under the trailer to pull it out. It was very heavy and about eighteen inches in diameter.

I couldn't see any damage to the undercarriage of the trailer, so I got the bathroom scale out of the camper and weighed the rock. It weighed eighty pounds!

I did find out later that the rock had damaged the cable on the emergency brake of the Suburban. A mechanic adjusted it for me and it was OK after that.

One night my wife and I pulled our Coachmen travel trailer into a campground just west of Mojave, California. After registering we were given directions to the site. It was as dark as pitch. We took off up a sand road, looking for the left turn we were supposed to make. The road was the same, exact color as the desert that surrounded it. It was almost impossible to tell the differenced between the road and the rest of the desert. I came to what I thought was a road that went up the side of a hill and I started up. A few yards up the road, I came to some deep ruts and pot holes and I knew that I was in the wrong place. I started to back the rig down the side of the hill.

My wife wanted to get out of the vehicle and guide me down the hill, but I thought that I could back down without a lot of trouble, so I just kept on backing. She kept insisting that she get out and guide me back onto the main road. Finally I relented and let her go. She took a flashlight and disappeared into the darkness. I sat there waiting for her directions. In a few moments the passenger door of the Suburban was pulled open

nd there stood my wife with eyes opened wide. "Don't back
p any more! You're backing off a cliff!" she said sternly.

I pulled up and stopped the rig and got out to see. It was
traight down! And just a few more feet and we would have
een history.

I got back into the truck and after a lot of maneuvering, finally
ot the rig turned around and we headed back to the office. I
nade the girl that had registered me, get on one of the golf carts
hat were parked by the guard shack and lead me to the camp
ite. She didn't want to at first, but I wasn't going by myself and I
onvinced her that she would have to either put me on a site or
ive me a refund. I guess it was easier to lead me to the camp
ite than it was to do the paper work for a refund.

I still try to be in the RV Park before dark, so I can see where
'm going, either forward or backward. *(if my wife would have*
hought about the possibility of there being snakes crawling around out
n the pitch dark I guess we would be writing about the time we drove
off a cliff in the California desert!)

We were in Anchorage, Alaska when we received word that
the newest member of our family, our grand daughter, had been
born in Baton Rouge, Louisiana. Meme and Pawpaw hitched up
and headed south. We drove the 4,568 miles to Baton Rouge in
only 12 days....lightning fast for us!

We were introduced to our new grand daughter, Lise' Claire
and we have been spending a lot of time in Louisiana. We can

hardly wait until she is big enough to come with Pawpaw and Meme on some motor home trips.....Mickey and Minnie loo out! Here we come!

I hope that this book has inspired you to get out and see som of this great country of ours. I pray that you have enjoye reading about some of the things that we did and the places w have visited.

That's it for now. I know that I'll have a more stories to te in the future, but until then.....***the adventure continues!!***

The End

Grand daughter, Lise' ready to hit the road in her new car.